OECD *Economic Surveys*
Electronic Books

The OECD, recognising the strategic role of electronic publishing, will be issuing the OECD *Economic Surveys*, both for the Member countries and for countries of Central and Eastern Europe covered by the Organisation's Centre for Co-operation with Economies in Transition, as electronic books with effect from the 1994/1995 series -- incorporating the text, tables and figures of the printed version. The information will appear on screen in an identical format, including the use of colour in graphs.

The electronic book, which retains the quality and readability of the printed version throughout, will enable readers to take advantage of the new tools that the ACROBAT software (included on the diskette) provides by offering the following benefits:

- ❑ User-friendly and intuitive interface
- ❑ Comprehensive index for rapid text retrieval, including a table of contents, as well as a list of numbered tables and figures
- ❑ Rapid browse and search facilities
- ❑ Zoom facility for magnifying graphics or for increasing page size for easy readability
- ❑ Cut and paste capabilities
- ❑ Printing facility
- ❑ Reduced volume for easy filing/portability

Working environment: DOS, Windows or Macintosh.

Subscription: FF 1 800   US$317   £200   DM 545

Single issue: FF 130   US$24   £14   DM 40

Complete 1994/1995 series on CD-ROM:

FF 2 000   US$365   £220   DM 600

Please send your order to OECD Electronic Editions or, preferably, to the Centre or bookshop with whom you placed your initial order for this Economic Survey.

OECD
ECONOMIC
SURVEYS

1994-1995

PORTUGAL

ORGANISATION FOR ECONOMIC CO-OPERATION AND DEVELOPMENT

ORGANISATION FOR ECONOMIC CO-OPERATION AND DEVELOPMENT

Pursuant to Article 1 of the Convention signed in Paris on 14th December 1960, and which came into force on 30th September 1961, the Organisation for Economic Co-operation and Development (OECD) shall promote policies designed:

— to achieve the highest sustainable economic growth and employment and a rising standard of living in Member countries, while maintaining financial stability, and thus to contribute to the development of the world economy;
— to contribute to sound economic expansion in Member as well as non-member countries in the process of economic development; and
— to contribute to the expansion of world trade on a multilateral, non-discriminatory basis in accordance with international obligations.

The original Member countries of the OECD are Austria, Belgium, Canada, Denmark, France, Germany, Greece, Iceland, Ireland, Italy, Luxembourg, the Netherlands, Norway, Portugal, Spain, Sweden, Switzerland, Turkey, the United Kingdom and the United States. The following countries became Members subsequently through accession at the dates indicated hereafter: Japan (28th April 1964), Finland (28th January 1969), Australia (7th June 1971), New Zealand (29th May 1973) and Mexico (18th May 1994). The Commission of the European Communities takes part in the work of the OECD (Article 13 of the OECD Convention).

Publié également en français.

3 2280 00481 3424

Table of contents

Boxes

Tables

Text

Diagrams

BASIC STATISTICS OF PORTUGAL

THE LAND

Area (thousand sq. km)	92.0	Major cities, resident population in thousands (1991):	
		Greater Lisbon	1 832
		Greater Oporto	1 153

THE PEOPLE

Population (1993, thousands)	9 350	Civilian employment (1994, thousands)	4 219
Number of inhabitants per sq. km	102	As a per centage of total:	
Civilian labour force (1994, thousands)	4 530	Agriculture	11.6
		Industry	33.0
		Services	55.4

PRODUCTION

Gross domestic product in 1993 (million of US$)	84 788	Gross domestic product at factor cost by origin (1990, per cent of total):	
Gross domestic product per head in 1993 (US$)	9 068	Agriculture	5.8
Gross fixed asset formation in 1993:		Industry	37.8
Per cent of GDP	25.1	Services	56.4
Per head (US$)	2 272		

THE GOVERNMENT

Public consumption (1993, per cent of GDP)	17.2	Composition of Parliament (number of seats):	
Public investment (1993, per cent of GDP)	4.2	Social Democrats (PSD)	135
(Per cent of total investment)	16.7	Socialists (PS)	72
General Government current revenue		Unified Democratic Coalition (CDU)	17
1993, per cent of GDP	37.6	Centre Social Democrats (CDS)	5
		National Solidarity (PSN)	1

FOREIGN TRADE

Exports of goods and services 1993, per cent of GDP	25.8	Imports of goods and services 1993, per cent of GDP	34.6
Main exports as a per centage of commodities exports, 1993 (SITC)		Main imports as a per centage of commodities imports, 1993 (SITC)	
Food, beverages and tobacco (0, 1)	6.8	Food, beverages and tobacco (0, 1)	12.3
Basic and semi-finished materials (2, 3, 4)	9.6	Basic and semi-finished materials (2, 3, 4)	13.6
Manufactured goods (5, 6, 7, 8)	83.5	Manufactured goods (5, 6, 7, 8)	74.1
of which: Chemicals (5)	4.4	of which: Chemicals (5)	9.7
Machinery and transport equipment (7)	21.1	Machinery and transport equipment (7)	35.8

THE CURRENCY

Monetary unit: Escudo		Currency units per US$, average of daily figures:	
		Year 1994	166.0
		March 1995	147.9

Note: An international comparison of certain basic statistics is given in an Annex table.

This survey is based on the Secretariat's study prepared for the annuel review of Portugal by the Economic and Development Review Committee on 22nd March 1995.

•

After revisions in the light of discussions during the review, final approval of the survey for publication was given by the Committee on 28th April 1995.

•

The previsous Survey of Portugal was issued in June 1994.

Introduction

The recession of 1993, which interrupted an eight-year spell of above OECD-average growth, has given way to an export-led expansion. Investment has begun to respond and as private consumption strengthens growth should accelerate in 1995. Wage moderation together with procyclical productivity gains have sharply curtailed the rise in unit labour costs, enabling inflation to abate further and providing a favourable basis for a sustainable recovery. Falling to 4 per cent in December 1994, the 12-month rate of consumer-price inflation has settled within the official target range, while the inflation gap with the EU has narrowed to 1 point. At the same time, macroeconomic policies have become more balanced. On the fiscal side, the budget deficit undershot the government target in 1994, falling to 5.8 per cent of GDP, 1.7 points lower than in 1993 when there was a large deficit overshoot. And the improving record on inflation and fiscal consolidation has enhanced the flexibility of monetary policy, which has been able to stabilise the nominal exchange rate while reducing interest rate differentials *vis-à-vis* Germany.

Nevertheless, despite prospects of further disinflation, market sentiment has remained volatile and the risk premium built into Portuguese interest rates is still large. The process of nominal convergence has thus been only partial so far. Moreover, compared with other countries, the 1993 recession was severe and the economic revival so far rather mild, with Portugal's output gains falling short of those of other countries. Making further progress towards convergence, with respect to financial conditions and real incomes, calls for the current policy consistency to be maintained over the medium run, not only with respect to macro-policy consolidation but also to further structural adjustment. For a country with a relatively low per capita income, notwithstanding significant catching-up in the last decade, policy options capable of speeding up real income convergence include both continued action to stimulate competition in the sheltered sector (discussed in the 1994 *Survey*) and programmes building on the improvements already made in Portuguese education and training systems.

The *Survey* begins with an examination of recent trends, including the forces accounting for Portugal's good unemployment record but relatively slow recovery. Macroeconomic and structural policies are analysed in Part II. The special chapter (Part III) deals with human capital and its role in economic convergence. A summary and Conclusions are presented in Part IV.

I. Recent developments and prospects

The recovery, which began in the first quarter of 1994, is taking place from a sounder basis than previous upturns. Inflation has converged towards the OECD Europe average, while the structural unemployment rate remains significantly below that in most other OECD economies. However, the business cycle has been more pronounced, with the annual rise in real GDP falling from 4.2 per cent in 1990 to 1.5 per cent in 1992 (Diagram 1); the subsequent slide into recession was also comparatively marked, with the level of output declining by 1.2 per cent in 1993 as against 0.1 per cent for OECD Europe as a whole.

In line with past upturns, the economy has been slower to pick up than elsewhere in Europe, real GDP being estimated to have progressed by only 1.2 per cent in 1994 as against an average output rebound of 2.4 per cent for OECD Europe. Thus, for the first time since accession to the European Community in 1986, Portugal's output growth has fallen behind the EU average for two consecutive years (Table 1). According to OECD projections, the negative growth differential should be virtually eliminated this year and become positive in 1996.

Measuring the extent to which output levels have diverged from those elsewhere in the EU has been complicated by a set of breaks in statistical data in 1992 and 1993.[1] The most important among these changes has been a revision of national accounts data, released in 1992.[2] These show Portugal's income level to have been systematically understated by around 13 per cent, of which two-thirds is accounted for by an under-recording of income from self-employment and one-third by counting incomes generated on the Azores and Madeira, previously excluded from the income statistics. Correspondingly, the new statistics reveal a smaller gap between income levels for the EU and Portugal (see Part III).

Diagram 1. **MACROECONOMIC PERFORMANCE**

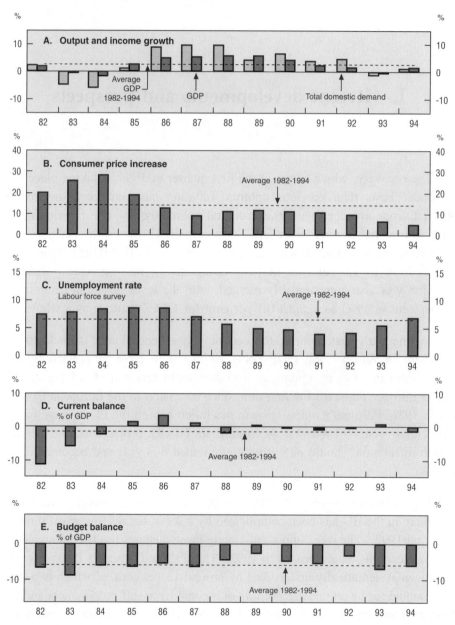

Source: OECD.

4

Table 1. **Macroeconomic indicators**

Percentage change

	1990	1991	1992	1993	1994[1]
Real GDP					
Portugal	4.2	2.2	1.5	–1.2	1.2
OECD Europe	3.2	1.5	1.2	–0.1	2.4
Total employment	2.3	3.0	0.9	–2.0	–0.1
Dependent employment	2.9	1.4	. .	–2.8	. .
Labour productivity	1.9	–0.8	0.6	1.0	1.7
Wages per employee[2]	17.2	14.2	13.8	6.9	4.8
Real wages per employee[3]	3.0	1.9	4.4	0.1	–0.5
Unit labour costs	15.3	15.2	13.4	5.9	3.0

1. Estimate.
2. Including supplementary benefits and employers' contributions to social security.
3. Deflated by the private consumption deflator.
Source: Bank of Portugal (1994), *Report for the Year 1993*, p. 28; data supplied by the Portuguese authorities.

Climbing out of the recession

The forces pulling down economic growth after 1990, the last year of the previous expansionary phase, were both internal and external:

– On the external side, the expansion in the volume of exports of goods subsided in 1991-93 in line with weaker market growth, although export market shares continued to rise throughout this period.

– Gross fixed investment, after surging at an annual 10 per cent rate in the 1986-90 period, lost most of its momentum in the early stages of the economic downswing and contracted sharply in absolute terms during the recession.

– Private consumption growth, having averaged 5.2 per cent a year in the 1986-90 period, fell to 0.4 per cent in 1993, the smallest gain in ten years.

The external sector acted increasingly as a drag on economic growth until 1993, when the volume of imports of goods and services contracted, while exports continued to grow moderately, cushioning the descent into recession (Diagram 2). Nevertheless, while economic growth recovered subsequently in

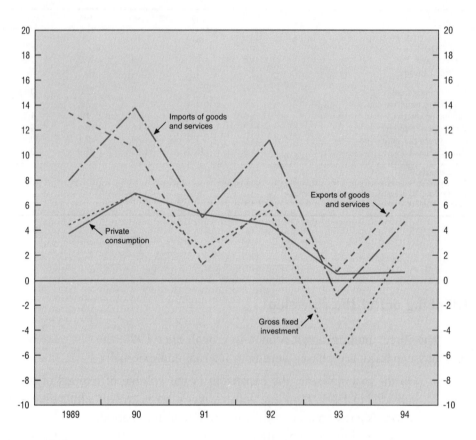

Diagram 2. **DEMAND COMPONENTS**

1985 prices, year-on-year percentage changes

Source: OECD.

Portugal's export markets, depressed domestic demand, notably private consumption, led to a widening of the negative differential between rates of real GDP growth for Portugal and OECD Europe.

The deceleration of private consumption growth since the early 1990s reflected an erosion of real wage gains and deteriorating job prospects. Real wages per employee stagnated in 1993 under the influence of falling dependent

Diagram 3. **INDUSTRIAL PRODUCTION AND BUSINESS INDICATORS**

Results of business surveys

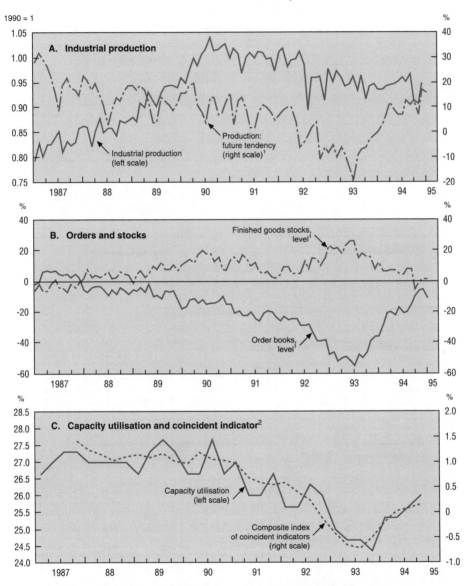

1. Per cent balance of positive and negative answers.
2. The coincident indicator measures changes in economic activity in trade, industry and construction.
Source: OECD.

Diagram 4. **CURRENT AND PREVIOUS RECOVERIES COMPARED**

Volume indices, trough = 100

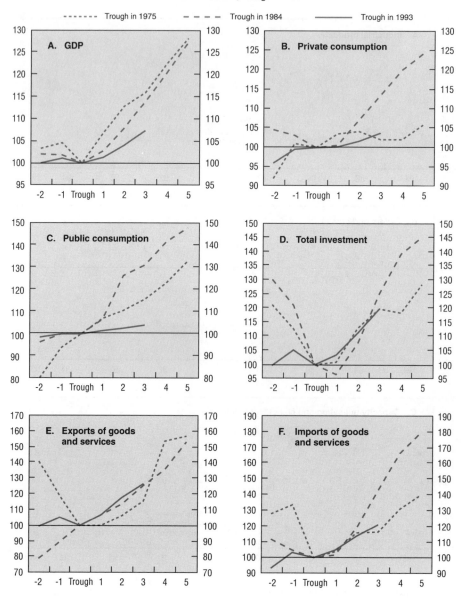

Source: OECD.

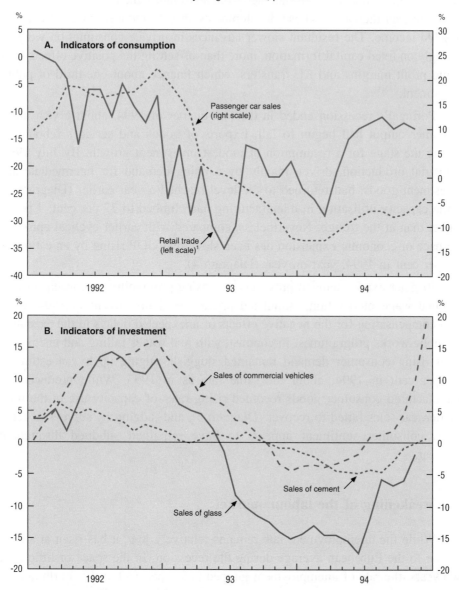

Diagram 5. **CONJONCTURAL INDICATORS OF DEMAND**

Year-on-year growth rate, per cent

A. **Indicators of consumption**

Passenger car sales
(right scale)

Retail trade
(left scale)[1]

B. **Indicators of investment**

Sales of commercial vehicles

Sales of cement

Sales of glass

1. Balance of positive and negative opinions.
Source: Bank of Portugal, *Monthly Bulletin.*

employment, and decreased in 1994 largely as a result of pay restraint in the public sector (Table 1). Real incomes from self-employment contracted in 1993, but recovered thereafter. These developments sharply reduced gains in real disposable income. The resultant slower advances in private consumption weighed strongly on fixed capital formation, more than offsetting the positive effects from rising profit margins and EU-transfers, which finance about one-third of public investment.

Portugal's recession ended in the first quarter of 1994, about a year and a half after output had begun to fall. Exports of goods and services rebounded, setting the stage for a resumption of modest investment growth. By July 1994, industrial production, driven mainly by a rising demand for intermediate and investment goods, had returned to the level reached a year earlier (Diagram 3), while capacity utilisation in manufacturing had climbed to 77 per cent, 4 points higher than at the trough. Nevertheless, compared with earlier cyclical episodes, the pace of economic expansion has been slow, real GDP rising by an estimated 1.2 per cent in 1994, year-on-year (Diagram 4).

Brighter export demand prospects and rising profitability, a consequence of nominal wage moderation, stimulated private fixed investment in 1994, more than compensating for the negative effects of unexpected delays in the execution of public works programmes. In contrast, with real wages falling and unemployment rising consumer demand remained sluggish, edging up by an estimated 0.5 per cent in 1994, about the same rate as in 1993. While producers of manufactured consumer goods recorded rising rates of capacity use in the third quarter, car sales failed to recover (Diagram 5), and judging by surveys of retail trade, consumer sentiment appears to have remained subdued throughout the year.

The weakening of the labour market

While the unemployment rate remains relatively low, it has risen at a pace similar to the European average during the recession. In the space of little over two years, the rate of unemployment jumped to 7.1 per cent in the fourth quarter of 1994, 3 points above the previous unemployment low in the second quarter of 1992 (Table 2). Many aspects of the labour market showed signs of serious deterioration: long-duration unemployment (twelve months and over) surged to

Table 2. **Labour-market indicators**

Percentages

	1990	1991	1992 [1]	1993	1994	1994			
						Q1	Q2	Q3	Q4
Labour force (growth rate)	1.9	2.4	..	−0.5	1.3	0.6	1.1	2.1	1.6
Male	1.2	1.0	..	−1.4	1.0	−0.4	0.3	2.2	1.7
Female	2.9	4.2	..	0.5	1.8	1.7	0.2	2.0	1.5
Employment (growth rate)	2.3	3.0	0.9	−2.0	−0.1	−1.3	−0.4	0.8	0.6
Male	1.4	1.4	..	−2.6	−0.5	−2.0	−1.1	−0.7	0.5
Female	3.5	5.1	..	−1.1	0.4	−0.5	0.4	1.0	0.7
Agriculture	−4.1	0.5	−2.3	−1.6	1.6	−1.2	1.5	3.2	3.1
Industry	0.9	0.3	−0.2	−2.7	−0.4	−1.7	−1.8	1.3	0.5
Services	6.0	5.9	2.3	−1.6	−0.2	−1.0	−0.1	0.1	0.1
Unemployment rate [2]	4.7	4.1	4.1	5.5	6.8	6.8	6.7	6.8	7.1
Male	3.2	2.8	3.4	4.7	6.0	5.8	5.9	6.2	6.3
Female	6.6	5.8	4.9	6.5	7.8	8.0	7.6	7.5	8.2
Youth	10.0	9.1	10.0	12.7	14.7	14.8	14.3	13.7	16.0
Long-term (12 months and over) [3]	34.7	30.0	26.8	29.3	34.1	33.4	33.4	35.9	33.9
Participation rate [4]	69.0	70.3	68.4	67.7	67.5	67.4	67.4	67.6	67.7
Male	80.5	80.7	78.7	77.1	76.4	76.4	76.3	76.6	76.3
Female	58.2	60.6	58.9	59.0	59.3	59.2	59.2	59.2	59.7
Job vacancies [2]	0.16	0.18	0.15	0.10	0.11	..	..	..	..

1. Break in series.
2. Per cent of labour force.
3. Per cent of total registered unemployment.
4. The working-age population is defined as 15 to 64 years old up to 1991 and as 16 to 64 years old afterwards.
Source: OECD, *Labour Force Statistics*; OECD, *Employment Outlook*; and Portuguese authorities.

over one-third of total registered unemployment in 1994 from 27 per cent in 1992; the youth unemployment rate climbed to a record high of 14.7 per cent; and the number of vacancies sank to a record low of 0.11 per cent of the labour force.

Dependent employment fell in all major sectors of the economy in 1993, with only a few subsectors (machinery and equipment, textiles, electricity, education and health) being spared employment losses. Labour shedding was more intense in industry, where male employment dominates, implying larger employment declines for men than for women (Table 2). The sex-specific employment trends continued to diverge in the initial phase of the economic recovery, with male employment declining until the third quarter of 1994, albeit at a reduced

11

rate, whereas the fall in female employment had already been reversed six months earlier. Nevertheless, the female unemployment rate in 1994 exceeded the male rate by the same margin as in 1993, as women entered the labour force in growing numbers, attracted by better job opportunities. Self-employment expanded in 1994, especially in agriculture and services.

Portugal has suffered broadly the same rise in unemployment over the past two years as other EU countries, although the recession has been more severe. Portugal retained its position as an economy with one of the best-performing labour markets. Its rate of unemployment in 1994 remained 5 points below the average for OECD Europe, and in contrast to most other OECD countries, non-cyclical unemployment, proxied by the rate of unemployment observed at the peak of the cycle, has drifted downward since the second oil price shock in 1979-80, a sign of enhanced labour market flexibility[3] (Diagram 6).

Portugal's labour market is generally viewed as being highly flexible: wage settlements and productivity gains are closely linked;[4] wage differentials across sectors widened in the 1982-92 period and are larger than in other European

Diagram 6. **RATE OF UNEMPLOYMENT**

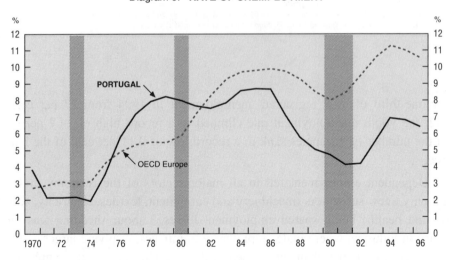

Note: Shaded area indicates cyclical peak.
Source: OECD.

12

Diagram 7. **LABOUR PRODUCTIVITY GROWTH: A CYCLICAL COMPARISON**[1]
Cyclical peak = 100

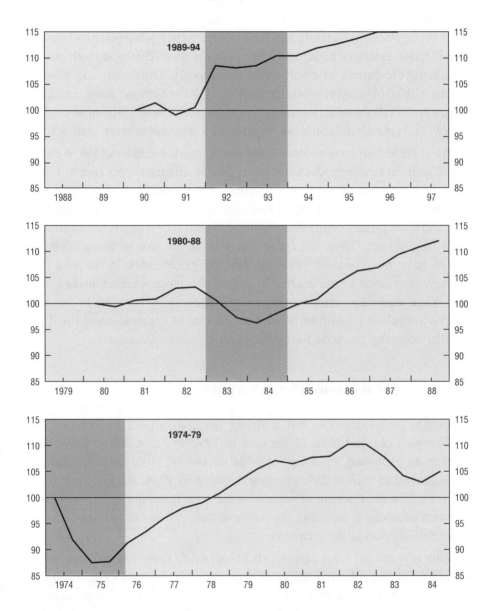

1. Shaded area indicates years of recession or slow economic growth.
Source: OECD.

13

countries; and disincentives to job search are limited, unemployment compensation being low in absolute terms and in relation to entry wages. Moreover, minimum wages adjusted for inflation fell more strongly in 1994 than the average wage.[5] While Portugal formerly had the most restrictive job protection legislation in the EU,[6] the easing of hiring and firing restrictions in 1989 and 1991[7] seems to have altered the pattern of employment adjustments. Dismissals and hirings of workers with a permanent work contract[8] may have become more sensitive to changes in overall demand, lessening the adjustment burden which, in a cyclical downswing, typically fell on workers without a permanent work contract.

As in other European countries, the labour market shake-out led to counter-cyclical gains in labour productivity, averaging an annual $1\frac{1}{2}$ per cent in 1993-94 (Table 1). Compared with previous cyclical downturns, such gains were a new phenomenon (Diagram 7), flowing from the greater freedom in adapting labour inputs and from greater competition in the sheltered sector as a result of structural reform (see below). Thus, the speed and size of the rise in unemployment in 1993-94 have no precedent since the first oil price shock in the mid-1970s. However, in relation to the decline in output, the labour market shake-out was mild. Wage equations show nominal wage growth in Portugal to be highly sensitive to cyclical conditions proxied by the rate of unemployment,[9] real wage flexibility reducing the need for cyclical employment adjustments.

Reduced wage- and consumer-price inflation

Surging unemployment had a strong negative impact on nominal wage growth, which plunged from 14 per cent in 1992 to 7 per cent in 1993, easing further to an estimated 5 per cent in 1994 (Table 1). In the process, real wage growth ground to zero in 1993, turning negative in 1994, the first such decline since 1988. The deceleration of nominal wages was quasi-universal, extending to all service subsectors, including the public sector. As was to be expected, strike activity fell off during the recession.

With no national wage agreements (*Accordo de Concertaçao*) concluded in 1993 and 1994, the collective nature of wage rises was in many cases diminished, the moderate wage outcomes for 1993 and 1994 concealing some variations across sectors, regions and skills. Wage rises implicit in collective wage settlements abated particularly strongly in the public sector, transport, storage, banking and insurance: partly reflecting these sectoral effects nominal wage growth weakened more markedly in the north than in the Lisbon area. The minimum wage in real terms (excluding domestic servants) contracted by an estimated 1.5 per cent in 1994, 1 point more than the average wage.

Together with counter-cyclical gains in productivity, nominal wage moderation cut the rise in unit labour costs from 13 per cent in 1992 to an estimated 3 per cent in 1994, the best result in nearly 30 years. At the onset of the recession, Portugal's unit labour costs were rising 6.7 points faster than the EU average, whereas in 1994, the gap shrank to around 3.1 points, contributing to continued inflation convergence. By December 1994, the 12-month rate of consumer-price inflation (excluding rent) stood at 4 per cent, the lowest rate in more than two decades, reducing the year-on-year rise to 5.2 per cent in 1994, within the official target range of 4 to 5.5 per cent (Diagram 8). At its December level, inflation was 5½ points lower than at the time when the economy began to slide into recession, and 1 point above the OECD Europe average. A rise in the standard VAT rate pushed up consumer-price inflation in the first two months of 1995.

Apart from the subdued rise in unit labour costs, the main force making for an unwinding of inflation has been greater price discipline imposed by the substantial real exchange rate appreciation which occurred in the 1991 to 1993 period. The change in the exchange-rate regime in October 1990 and the subsequent entry of the escudo into the wide band of the ERM in April 1992 increasingly constrained the ability of producers to raise prices.[10] With exports and imports of goods and services representing, respectively, marginally less and more than 30 per cent of GDP, exchange rate changes are of prime importance in shaping inflation. In 1993, increases in VAT rates for goods temporarily reversed disinflation in the tradeables[11] sector. However, the most remarkable characteristic of 1994 was the sharply weaker trend in price rises for non-tradeables, partly reflecting more intense competition in the domain of retail sales and financial services. As a result, the inflation differential between the open and sheltered sectors, which was criticised in the 1994 *Survey* as slowing down the process of inflation convergence, narrowed substantially (Diagram 9).

Diagram 8. **INFLATION DEVELOPMENTS**
Year-on-year percentage changes

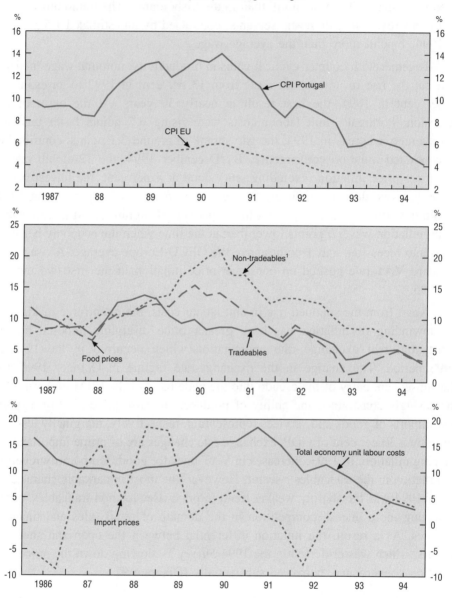

1. Including services and construction.
Source: Bank of Portugal and OECD.

16

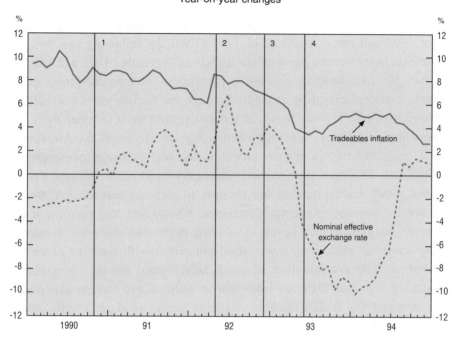

Diagram 9. **TRADEABLES INFLATION AND THE NOMINAL EXCHANGE RATE**

Year-on-year changes

1. October 1990, abolition of downward crawling peg-system.
2. April 1992, entry into wide band of ERM.
3. November 1992, 1st Escudo devaluation.
4. May 1993, 2nd Escudo devaluation.
Source: Bank of Portugal and OECD.

International competitiveness and the balance of payments

The trade balance has strengthened over the past two years, the deficit narrowing from 9.9 per cent of GDP in 1992 to an estimated 7.0 per cent of GDP in 1994. While currency depreciation sharply reduced the terms of trade, export volumes expanded strongly during 1994 while the relative weakness of domestic demand has damped the recovery of imports.

17

The fall in the nominal and real exchange rate

The nominal effective exchange rate fell by 6.5 per cent between the first half of 1992 and the second half of 1994 (Table 3), following two downward adjustments in the central parity of the escudo in November 1992 and May 1993 (see Part II). Measured by relative export prices in manufacturing, the real exchange rate depreciated by a smaller amount, the decline more than offsetting the cumulative loss in price competitiveness incurred since October 1990, when the crawling peg policy was abandoned (Diagram 10, Panel B). Measured by relative unit labour costs in manufacturing, the real exchange rate appreciated marginally, as exporters seem to have accepted cuts in profit margins. Prices of imported goods reacted quickly and strongly to currency depreciation. But with the domestic economy flagging, Portuguese wholesalers and retailers reduced their profit margins, so that the rise in inflation in the tradeables sector, measured by the consumer price index, was mild compared with the size of currency depreciation. The configuration of price adjustments flowing from currency depreciation was thus different from that in Italy, where foreign exporters cut prices destined for Italian markets, while domestic producers were quick in raising export prices.[12]

Table 3. **Currency depreciation and foreign trade prices**

1992 I = 100

	1992	1993		1994	
	II	I	II	I	II
Nominal effective exchange rate	101.0	99.7	92.6	91.7	93.5
Import prices	111.0	108.8	113.6	115.0	116.7
Export prices	101.3	102.2	109.3	108.7	109.9
Relative export prices	101.2	98.8	93.3	94.3	95.6
Relative unit labour costs	97.4	102.5	93.2	99.5	101.4
Relative consumer prices	103.1	101.7	95.7	95.8	97.9
Consumer prices	105.0	111.9	109.2	115.0	117.6

Source: OECD estimates.

Diagram 10. **NOMINAL AND REAL EXCHANGE RATES**
1987 = 100

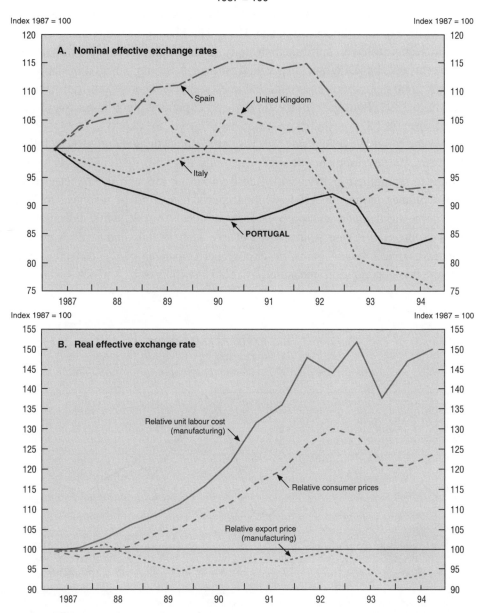

Source: OECD.

19

The response of trade volumes

The trade balance has improved since 1992, as import volumes plunged in 1993, while export volumes surged in 1994. The change in the relative cyclical position seems to have contributed strongly to this improvement. Its importance is brought out by Diagram 11, which shows a strong correlation between Portugal's real net exports and relative domestic demand conditions in the OECD area. Up to 1992, Portugal's domestic demand expanded much faster than in the rest of the OECD, pushing up imports relative to exports. However, in 1993-94 the relative cyclical position reversed, domestic demand growth falling behind foreign developments. It was principally this shift that caused net export volumes to strengthen in 1993-94.[13] Led by a strong rebound in market growth, export volumes surged in 1994, while imports recovered in response to both rising domestic demand and stronger foreign sales. Overall, while Portugal has gained export market shares since 1992 (Table 4), both Italy and Spain were able to achieve much larger gains in export performance, partly reflecting real exchange rate depreciation (measured by relative export prices) which was nearly

Diagram 11. **NET EXPORTS AND THE CYCLE**
1987 = 100

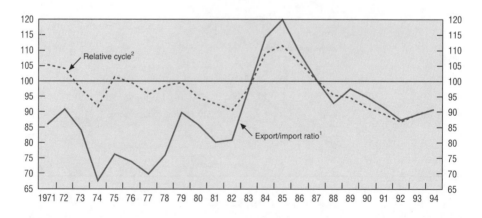

1. Index of exports divided by the index of imports of goods, at constant prices.
2. Index of domestic demand of OECD countries (excluding Portugal) divided by the index of Portuguese demand at constant prices.
Source: OECD.

Table 4. **Currency depreciation and manufacturing export performance, 1994**

Index: 1992 = 100

	Portugal	Italy	United Kingdom	Spain
Nominal effective exchange rate	92.1	80.9	92.2	83.0
Relative unit labour costs	101.7	79.9	93.7	84.3
Relative export prices	94.4	88.5	103.0	89.7
Export performance [1]	106.2	116.6	100.8	126.9
Implicit elasticity of export performance with respect to decline in relative export prices	1.11	1.44	..	2.61

1. Ratio of export volumes to export market growth.
Source: OECD estimates.

twice as large as that apparent for Portugal. However, the implicit response of Portuguese export volumes with respect to shifts in the real exchange rate has also been less strong. This outcome may be associated with a lack of efficient distribution channels abroad and inadequate brand advertising[14] as well as with reduced profit margins on export goods. The resultant lack of marketing ability may make it difficult to switch output from domestic to foreign markets when domestic demand contracts.

The current and capital accounts

A lower trade deficit, along with higher receipts from tourism and transfers, shifted the current account into surplus to the amount of 0.8 per cent of GDP on a transaction basis in 1993 (Table 5), the best result since 1989. This improvement was transitory, however, as a steep fall in transfers, both private and public, more than offset a further improvement in the goods account, shifting the current account back into deficit to the extent of 1.3 per cent of GDP. Net official transfers were reduced by higher mandatory payments to the EU, a consequence of the upward revision of national income data, and lower receipts from the EU, reflecting delays in the implementation of co-financed investment projects. The decline in private transfers, mainly emigrants' remittances, reflected depressed labour markets abroad.

The capital account (excluding banks, but including unrecorded transactions) closed with a surplus in 1993 (Table 5), as non-residents, attracted by prospects of falling short-term interest rates and associated capital gains, bought

Table 5. **Balance of payments**

Billion escudos

	1990	1991	1992	1993	1994 [1]
Exports (fob)	2 320	2 339	2 450	2 685	2 853
Imports (fob)	3 287	3 473	3 732	3 788	3 874
Trade balance	−968	−1 134	−1 281	−1 103	−1 021
Services, net	160	171	209	145	69
Investment income, net	−34	11	90	−7	−22
Transfers, net	782	868	1 059	1 077	780
Private	638	666	643	619	481
Public	144	202	414	458	299
Current balance	−26	−96	−23	112	−194
(as a per cent of GDP)	(−0.3)	(−1.0)	(−0.2)	(0.8)	(−1.3)
Medium- and long-term capital, net	511	587	−45	207	..
Basic balance	485	492	−68	340	..
Short-term capital and unrecorded transactions, net	80	263	140	−149	..
Balance on non-monetary transactions	565	754	72	191	..
Short-term capital of private monetary institutions, net	−47	113	−71	−619	405
Balance on official settlements	518	868	1	−428	−310

1. Preliminary data.
Source: Data supplied by the Portuguese authorities.

large amounts of domestic securities, notably shares and fixed-rate government bonds. However, in 1994 portfolio investment by non-residents posted a deficit mainly reflecting unfavourable developments in international bond markets. Even so, the overall capital account (including the short-term net external position of banks) showed a surplus in 1994, dampening the fall in official external reserves.

The outlook to 1996

The main assumptions behind the short-term projection concern the buoyancy of the international environment and domestic economic policy restraint. The assumptions regarding the international environment imply an increasingly robust recovery in Europe, where growth may settle at 3 per cent from mid-1995 and onwards, together with a slowdown in the United States. For

Portugal, these projections imply that export market growth is likely to ease to 8 to 9 per cent in 1995 and 1996. Underlying the projections are technical assumptions of unchanged exchange rates as of 2nd May 1995 which in the case of Portugal implies a stable effective exchange rate from the first half of 1995, and an average OECD import price of oil which rises with the general rate of inflation.

OECD projections are based on the assumption that the government will allow the general government borrowing requirement to fall below its target of 5.8 per cent of GDP in 1995. Monetary policy continues to be geared towards achieving inflation convergence with the best performing EU countries, the stability of the nominal exchange rate remaining the key intermediate target. In this setting, risk premia in domestic interest rates could narrow, but the process could be slow, given the slow scheduled pace of fiscal consolidation.

Table 6. **Short-term projections** [1]

Percentage changes

	1990	1991	1992	1993	1994	1995	1996
Demand and output							
Private consumption	7.0	4.8	3.7	0.4	0.2	1.3	2.1
Public consumption	5.7	3.0	1.4	0.0	1.4	1.1	1.5
Gross fixed investment	6.8	2.4	5.4	−4.8	3.5	7.5	7.8
Final domestic demand	6.7	3.5	3.8	−1.0	1.2	2.9	3.6
Stockbuilding [2]	−0.2	0.4	0.6	0.2	0.0	0.4	−0.0
Total domestic demand	6.5	4.2	4.3	−0.9	1.2	3.2	3.5
Exports of goods and services	10.5	0.5	6.1	−5.1	6.7	10.5	7.3
Imports of goods and services	13.7	5.4	11.1	−3.2	4.6	8.4	6.5
Foreign balance [2]	−3.1	−2.8	−4.0	−0.1	−0.2	−1.0	−1.1
GDP at market prices	4.3	2.1	1.1	−1.2	1.2	2.9	3.2
Prices							
GDP price deflator	13.0	15.5	13.5	7.4	5.0	4.5	4.4
Private consumption deflator	11.7	12.5	10.0	7.9	5.2	4.5	4.2
Unemployment (per cent of total labour force)	4.7	4.1	4.2	5.5	6.8	6.7	6.3

1. May 1995.
2. As a percentage of GDP in the previous period.
Source: OECD.

23

Against this background, economic growth may accelerate in 1995 spurred by a continued expansion of export markets, the coming on-stream of new export capacity[15] and stronger fixed investment. Consumer demand may firm with the brightening of employment prospects, reinforcing the domestic stimulus to output growth in 1996 (Table 6).

The projected strengthening of economic activity will gradually reduce the unemployment rate but the projected rate of 6.3 per cent in 1996, would still be marginally above the estimated NAIRU. The consequent deceleration of nominal wages would enable consumer-price inflation to settle in the upper half of the new target range of 3.5 to 4.5 per cent. On the external side, rising transfer payments may shift the current account back into balance in 1995-96, outweighing a cyclically-induced deterioration of the trade account.

The main risks to the outlook concern interest rates, the exchange rate and fiscal consolidation. Renewed turbulence in financial markets might put downward pressure on the escudo, driving up interest rates. Investors' attitudes have remained cautious following the latest escudo devaluation, making it imperative that any unexpected revenue buoyancy be used to reduce the budget deficit rather than raise expenditures, 1995 being an election year.

II. Macroeconomic and structural policies

Overview

The commitment to a stable exchange rate has remained the centre-piece of Portugal's strategy of economic convergence. With inflation falling and the budgetary situation improving, the nominal effective exchange rate has appreciated since mid-1994. In this setting, the Bank of Portugal was able to resume its policy of cautious interest rate reductions in July (Diagram 12). Long-term bond yields, though, continued to suffer from the change in sentiment in international markets, the differential with Germany widening to around 4.5 points in early 1995 and to 5 points in April. Although fiscal consolidation in 1994 proceeded more rapidly than planned, following the large deficit overshoot of the previous year, the fiscal deficit is still significantly above the 3 per cent Maastricht criterion. Overall, however, the trend towards a more balanced stance of macroeconomic policy has improved the prospects for securing full participation in the EU's plans for economic and monetary union, Portugal's main objective over the medium run. Moreover, consolidation efforts are being supported by a programme of structural reform within the context of the single market.

Monetary and exchange-rate policy

The exchange rate and monetary policy

Portugal has been a member of the Exchange Rate Mechanism of the EMS since April 1992, and with capital movements freed from all restrictions since December 1992, exchange-rate stability became the primary intermediate target of monetary policy. Given the weak state of the economy in 1993-94, the Bank of Portugal sought, where consistent with this primary objective, to steer interest rates down.[16] But, overall, following the reform of the ERM in August 1993,

Diagram 12. **EXCHANGE-RATE AND INTEREST-RATE DEVELOPMENTS**

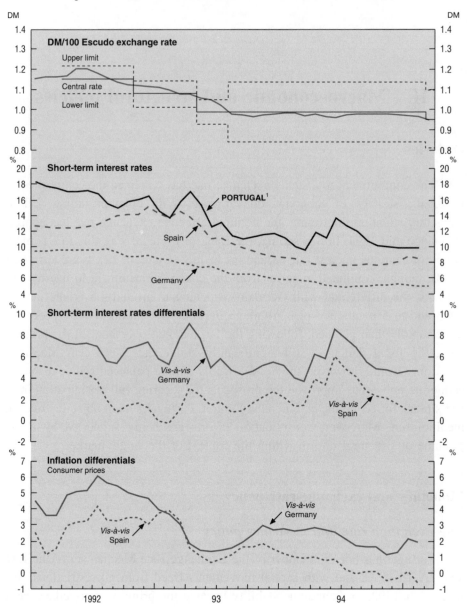

DM/100 Escudo exchange rate

Upper limit
Central rate
Lower limit

Short-term interest rates

PORTUGAL[1]

Spain

Germany

Short-term interest rates differentials

Vis-à-vis
Germany

Vis-à-vis
Spain

Inflation differentials
Consumer prices

Vis-à-vis
Germany

Vis-à-vis
Spain

1992   93   94

1. 3-month Interbank money market rate (86 to 96 days).
Source: OECD.

Diagram 13. **ESCUDO EXCHANGE RATES**
1990 = 100

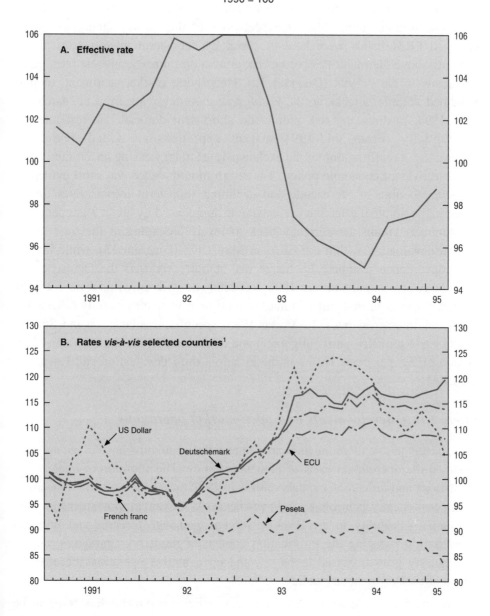

A. Effective rate

B. Rates *vis-à-vis* selected countries[1]

US Dollar

Deutschemark

ECU

French franc

Peseta

1. Escudos per unit of foreign currency.
Source: OECD estimates.

keeping the escudo within previous intervention limits required the Bank of Portugal to maintain a firmer monetary stance than might have been called for on domestic grounds alone. Market expectations of the escudo sliding within the enlarged ERM bands were held in check by short-term interest rates almost 6 points above German rates before risk premia on domestic interest rates began to narrow in early 1994 (Diagram 12). Underlying market sentiment, though, remained volatile: attacks on the Portuguese currency reoccurred in March and May 1994, pushing the risk premia on short-term domestic interest rates up substantially. From mid-1994 market apprehensions faded again, the government's reaffirmation of the exchange rate strategy easing uncertainty about the objectives of economic policy. The return of confidence was most evident in the strengthening of the escudo and declining short-term interest rates. In the process, the nominal effective exchange rate appreciated by about 3 per cent over the summer, taking the currency back to levels prevailing at the time of the second devaluation within the ERM in May 1993 (Diagram 13), while interest rate convergence resumed. Exchange rate stability *vis-à-vis* the Deutschemark over the twelve months to mid-1994 was achieved with only minor net losses in official reserves so that shifts in market sentiment were almost fully reflected in variations in interest rates. In March 1995, speculative attacks on the Spanish peseta led to an ERM-parity alignment and a reduction in the central value of the escudo of 3.5 per cent. This was the escudo's third devaluation since it joined the ERM.

Interest rate developments and open-market operations

Exchange-rate targeting and rapid financial deregulation have in recent years modified the operational basis of monetary policy. The abolition of interest rate regulations and remaining capital controls in 1992 meant the gradual replacement of direct monetary controls by indirect means. With capital movements causing substantial instability in the level of foreign exchange reserves and financial liberalisation reducing the information content of monetary aggregates, targets for liquidity growth ceased to be set, and open market operations became the principal tool of monetary policy.

In the process, a set of new monetary policy instruments has come to be developed, facilitating the pursuit of the exchange rate objective. The "overnight credit facility", introduced in July 1993, is a standing facility for the provision of liquidity (at a penalty rate). Under normal market conditions, the rate on this facility sets the ceiling for very short-term money market rates, while the rate on the "standing facility for the absorption of liquidity" acts as a floor. Both rates are useful in signalling changes in the monetary policy stance. Under exceptional money market circumstances, like foreign exchange market turbulence, the overnight credit facility was temporarily suspended. Very short-term money market rates are steered within the band via "variable rate repos", introduced in July 1994, and this instrument provides a more effective means of adapting intervention in the money market to management of the exchange rate. From June 1994, this rate has settled within the range defined by the daily facility and the absorption rate. With confidence in the escudo returning, minimum and maximum rates were lowered in several steps, and the variable rate repos dropped from a peak of 13.8 per cent in June to below 9 per cent in December (Diagram 14).

Interest paid on compulsory reserves having been cut to 8.75 per cent in October 1994, the authorities reformed the system of minimum reserve requirements in November, in line with recent EU guidelines. The compulsory reserves

Diagram 14. **KEY OFFICIAL INTEREST RATES**

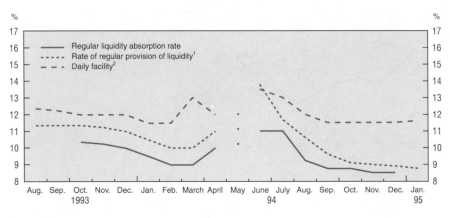

* = Suspended.
1. Regular operations for liquidity injection are contracted on the first working day of each reserve maintenance period and mature in the first working day of the subsequent period. From May 1994 variable rate on repurchase-agreements.
2. Standing facility, based on pre-anounced rate liquidity provision operations maturing on the next working day following the transaction. Use of this facility is automatic.
Source: Bank of Portugal, *Monthly Bulletin.*

Diagram 15. **INTEREST RATES**

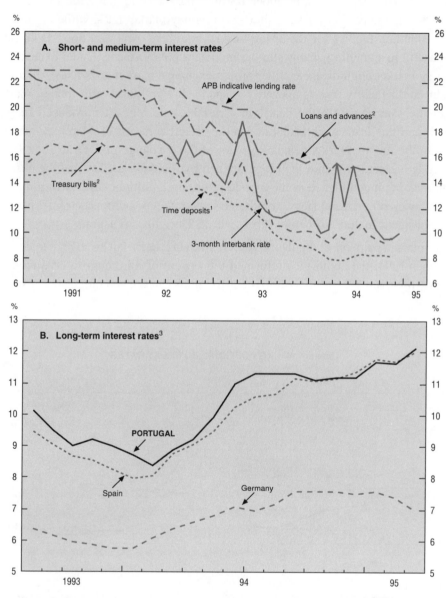

A. **Short- and medium-term interest rates**

APB indicative lending rate

Loans and advances[2]

Treasury bills[2]

Time deposits[1]

3-month interbank rate

B. **Long-term interest rates[3]**

PORTUGAL

Spain

Germany

1.   181 days up to one year.
2.   91 days up to 180 days.
3.   10-year government bonds.
Source: Bank of Portugal and OECD.

30

coefficient was reduced from 17 per cent (partially remunerated) to 2 per cent (non-remunerated), releasing liquidity of around Esc 1 900 billion, which was absorbed via issues of central bank certificates of deposit (CD) with maturities ranging from two to ten years. Banks are allowed to use these CDs as collateral in repo-transactions or as contributions to a deposit guarantee fund established in January 1995. The Bank of Portugal also extended to 1997 the deadline for banks to build up reserves for covering pension liabilities.

The cuts in official interest rates since June 1994 have been mirrored in the three-month interbank rate, which, after surging to 13.8 per cent in June, dropped to 10.6 in December (Diagram 15). In the process the differential *vis-à-vis* Germany narrowed sharply. By February 1995 it had reached 5 points, compared with 8.5 points cent in June 1994. Rates applied to best customers (CRISTAL) also fell, but the decline has been less pronounced for some corporate interest rates, reflecting the augmented default risk attaching to some companies, given the rise in non-performing loans.

In the capital market, yields on 10-year Treasury bonds jumped by nearly 3 points in the spring of 1994, a shift triggered by the turmoil in world bond markets, but which affected Portuguese yields more than the average. They remained at that level in the second half of the year, but edged up further in early 1995 amid enhanced political uncertainties in Spain and renewed disturbances in world bond markets related to the Mexican crisis: in February 1995, the rate on 10-year government bonds, at 11.65 per cent, was $3\frac{1}{2}$ percentage points higher than the low reached in February 1994, and $4\frac{1}{4}$ points above the German equivalent. This differential widened further in the wake of the escudo devaluation in March, reaching 5 points in April.

Evolution of money and credit

The growth of credit to firms and individuals was slow to reflect the cyclical downturn of the economy. At a time when the level of output was already falling, private credit growth was still buoyant, fuelled by structural forces including the removal of restrictions on consumer credit and increased bank competition in the mortgage market. It was only from the second half of 1993 that the expansion of credit to firms and individuals slackened (Diagram 16). In December 1994, the 12-month rate of private credit growth stood at 10.8 per cent compared with 17.2 per cent a year earlier.

Diagram 16. MONETARY AND CREDIT AGGREGATES

Year-on-year percentage changes

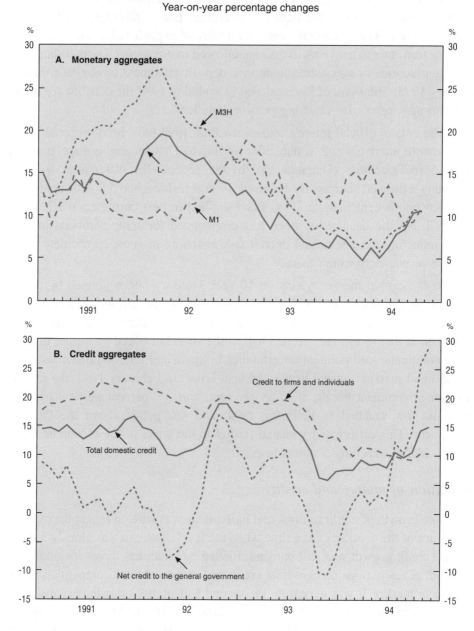

A. Monetary aggregates

M3H

L-

M1

B. Credit aggregates

Credit to firms and individuals

Total domestic credit

Net credit to the general government

Source: Bank of Portugal.

Liquidity growth continued to abate in 1993 and the first half of 1994, curbed by the slower pace of credit expansion and a negative contribution from the external side. Outflows of short-term capital and the deficit on current account reduced official reserves (see Part I). Growth in L- (liquid assets held in Portugal by the non-financial sector) sank to a low of 4.6 per cent in May, down from 6.6 per cent in December 1993 and 13 per cent in December 1992 (Diagram 16). However, over the six months to September 1994 the expansion of domestic liquidity suddenly gathered speed, largely driven by a switch from bonds to liquid assets, mostly time deposits and deposits denominated in foreign currency.[17]

Fiscal policy

The 1994 budget outturn

The 1994 fiscal outcome was significantly better than projected, as surging tax revenues combined with spending restraint to outweigh the adverse effects of higher-than-expected interest payments, social security expenditure and lower net receipts from the European Community budget. The general government borrowing requirement fell to an estimated 5.8 per cent of GDP from 7.5 per cent in 1993, about one point lower than expected[18] (Table 7). Structural measures, including the closing of tax loopholes in 1993, better compliance with tax rules and a more efficient monitoring of tax liabilities, contributed to the deficit reduction.[19] As a result, in cyclically-adjusted terms, the budget deficit is estimated to have narrowed, falling below 5 per cent in 1994.

According to national accounts data, current receipts climbed to 39 per cent of GDP in 1994, while current outlays, mainly reflecting lower interest payments and public pay restraint posted a smaller rise (Table 7). A four point decline in the effective rate of interest on domestic public debt – the lagged effect of the fall in interest rates in 1992-93 – was instrumental in reducing interest payments in terms of GDP, more than offsetting expenditure effects from further debt accretion (Diagram 17). Within total outlays, capital spending fell relative to GDP, as EU-co-financed investment projects[20] were slow in being executed.

Table 7. **General government accounts**

Billion escudos

| | Estimated outcome | | 1995 budget |
	1993	1994	
Current receipts	4 888.7	5 689.7	6 127.9
In per cent of GDP	35.9	39.0	39.0
Taxes and social security contributions	4 097.6	4 537.2	4 798.5
Other	791.1	1 152.5	1 329.4
Current expenditure	5 372.6	6 003.1	6 479.5
In per cent of GDP	39.4	41.1	41.2
Interest payments	930.3	812.2	835.9
Current balance	−483.9	−313.4	−351.6
Capital receipts	487.2	490.4	606.4
Capital expenditure	1 019.5	1 021.0	1 164.3
Capital balance	−532.3	−530.6	−557.9
Total overall balance	−1 016.2	−844.0	−909.5
In per cent of GDP	−7.5	−5.8	−5.8

Source: Data on public accounts (cash basis) supplied by the Portuguese authorities.

On the revenue side, stepped-up efforts to rein in tax evasion boosted VAT receipts, which reached 7.1 per cent of GDP, a record high (Table 8). The revenue share of direct taxes remained broadly unchanged at 8 per cent of GDP. In contrast, net receipts from EU transfers fell sharply from 1993-levels, reduced by the twin influence of higher contributions to the EU-budget (a consequence of revised national income data) and delayed transfers from the EU (Table 9).

Comparing budget outcomes at different levels of government shows a substantial deficit cut for the central administration (including autonomous funds, but excluding transfers to social security and local authorities), going far beyond the targeted deficit reduction. This positive result mainly reflected the greater efficiency in collecting indirect taxes, more stringent public pay restraint, higher payments by civil servants to the public pension fund and improved debt management. Amounting to 1.8 per cent of GDP, the deficit undershoot for the central administration reversed the severe fiscal setback of the previous year. In

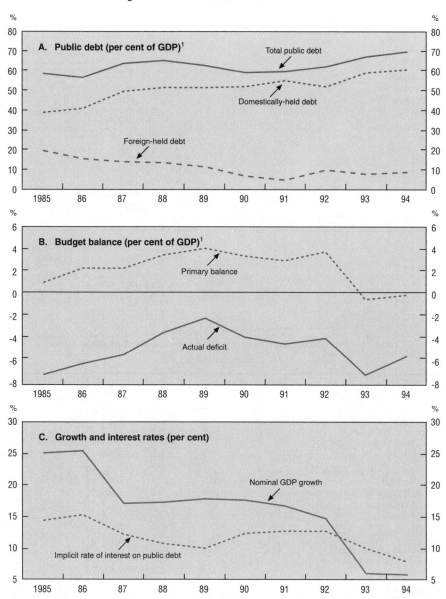

Diagram 17. **PUBLIC DEBT DEVELOPMENTS**

A. Public debt (per cent of GDP)[1]

Total public debt

Domestically-held debt

Foreign-held debt

B. Budget balance (per cent of GDP)[1]

Primary balance

Actual deficit

C. Growth and interest rates (per cent)

Nominal GDP growth

Implicit rate of interest on public debt

1. Per cent of GDP. Based on new national accounts data.
Source: OECD.

Table 8. **State tax receipts**

Per cent of GDP

	1991	1992	1993	1994 Estimated outcome	1995 Budget
Direct taxation	8.4	9.2	8.2	8.0	7.8
Personal income	5.4	6.6	6.1	6.0	5.7
Corporate income	2.6	2.5	2.0	2.0	2.0
Other	0.4	0.1	0.1	0.1	0.1
Indirect taxation	12.1	13.0	12.2	13.5	13.1
Fuel tax	2.8	2.8	2.7	2.7	2.8
Value added tax	5.7	6.5	5.9	7.1	7.1
Car tax	0.6	0.8	0.7	0.8	0.9
Tobacco tax	0.8	0.8	1.0	1.0	1.0
Stamp tax	1.7	1.6	1.6	1.5	1.1
Other	0.6	0.5	0.3	0.4	0.3
Total	20.5	22.2	20.4	21.5	20.9

Source: Data supplied by the Portuguese authorities.

Table 9. **Public transfers between Portugal and the European Union**

Billion escudos

	1991	1992	1993	January-August	
				1993	1994
1. From Portugal to the European Union	130.2	146.3	162.9	109.5	183.3
Financial contribution	88.7	108.7	127.5	85.0	153.4
Customs and levelling duties	37.7	36.6	35.4	24.5	29.5
Other	3.8	1.0	0.0		0.4
2. From the European Union to Portugal	300.8	557.4	619.3	428.5	381.2
Reimbursement of financial contribution	8.4	0.3	0.0		
EAGGF-guarantee [1]	56.6	74.4	86.4	59.1	98.8
EAGGF-guidance [2]	41.3	64.3	61.8	33.9	37.3
ERDF [3]	147.3	275.5	286.0	224.5	157.7
ESF [4]	26.6	115.9	152.8	97.3	52.7
PEDIP – specific budget [5]	20.3	21.2	10.8	7.5	5.5
Social cohesion fund			15.7	5.7	26.5
Other	0.3	5.8	5.8	0.6	2.6
3. Balance (2-1)	170.6	411.1	456.4	319.0	197.9

1. European Agricultural Guidance and Guarantee Fund – Guarantee.
2. European Agricultural Guidance and Guarantee Fund – Guidance.
3. European Regional Development Fund.
4. European Social Fund.
5. Specific Programme for the Development of Portuguese Industry – specific budget.
Source: Directorate-General of the Treasury.

36

Table 10. **General government deficit**

Per cent of GDP[1]

	1993	1994		1995
		Target	Estimated outcome	
General government[2]	7.5	6.9	5.8	5.8
Central government[3]	3.7	3.4	1.6	1.7
Regional and local authorities	2.2	1.5	2.1	1.8
Social security	1.6	2.0	2.1	2.3

1. Based upon revised national accounts data.
2. "Sector publico administrativo" (public accounts basis, including autonomous funds).
3. Including autonomous funds.
Source: Ministerio das Finanças (1994), *Relatório do Orçamento do Estado para 1995*, pp. 60-61, and data supplied by the Portuguese authorities.

contrast, deficit overruns occurred at other levels of government, notably among regional and local authorities, damping the tempo of fiscal consolidation (Table 10).

Public debt and debt management

The rate of public debt accretion slowed in 1994, as the primary balance strengthened and the gap between the implicit rate on interest on public debt and nominal income growth narrowed (Diagram 17, Panel B). Public debt moved up from 67 to 70 per cent of GDP, still below the EU average (Diagram 17). Debt accumulation would have been smaller had privatisation proceeds, part of which were earmarked for debt redemption,[21] not fallen short of target, a consequence of depressed conditions on stock and bond markets.

Following the removal of capital controls in 1992, public debt management has sought to establish a regular presence of Portugal in international markets, creating benchmarks for Portuguese bonds. During 1993 and 1994 lower interest rates prevailing abroad stimulated greater recourse to foreign funding, pushing the foreign public debt up to an estimated 9.3 per cent of GDP in 1994. This was about twice as high as in 1991, prior to the escudo entering the ERM, but lower than in several other OECD economies.[22] Domestically-held debt changed little in terms of GDP. Moreover, with the overall debt level expanding, debt manage-

Table 11. **State sector borrowing requirement in 1994**

Billion escudos

	Budget proposal	Estimated outcome
State budget deficit	779.0	725.1
Financial transactions		
Liquid financial assets	6.1	−1.1
Credit extended to social security	118.0	118.0
Adjustment of public debt[1]	238.0	221.9
Privatisation proceeds[2]	−80.0	−50.2
Public sector borrowing requirement	1 061.1	1 013.7
Financing		
Treasury bills	0	343.3
External credit	302.6	384.9
Other[3]	758.5	285.5

1. Incorporation into public debt of liabilities incurred by public enterprises (*regulaizações de dívidas*).
2. Negative equals sales.
3. Medium and long-term domestic securities, including reduction in financial balances (*utilização de saldos de empréstimos de anos anteriores*).

Source: Ministerio das Finanças (1994), *Relatório do Orçamento do Estado para 1995*, p. 71.

ment policies continued to be directed at smoothing and lengthening the maturity structure of government liabilities and lowering their effective interest rate. To this end, the government for the first time issued a global ECU loan (February 1994), diversified maturities, reduced the share of non-marketable debt instruments and further enhanced the efficiency of the capital market through structural reform measures (see below). However, stepping up sales of fixed rate marketable instruments proved difficult. Faced with a steepening yield curve, the government increasingly switched to issues of Treasury bills, which covered an estimated 34 per cent of the total public borrowing requirement in 1994 (Table 11). As a result, the average maturity of the domestic marketable debt fell from 3.06 years at the end of 1993 to 2.71 years at the end of September 1994. Recourse to external credit was close to the limit set by the 1994 budget, providing for nearly 38 per cent of financial needs.

The 1995 budget and the medium-term consolidation programme

The 1995 budget projects a general government borrowing requirement of Esc 909 billion or 5.8 per cent of GDP (Table 7). Public debt is projected to edge up to 72 per cent of GDP, partly driven by the incorporation into public debt of financial liabilities incurred by TAP, the State-owned national carrier, and Siderurgia Nacional, the State-owned steel company. The budget modifies the structure of overall spending and revenues, cuts in direct taxation and social security contributions being offset by higher indirect taxes, while capital outlays are set to be raised sharply following underspending in 1994. Underlying the budget are projections of real GDP growth accelerating to 2½ to 3½ per cent from an estimated 1 per cent in 1994 and inflation settling within the new target range of 3.5 to 4.5 per cent.

In the State sector, current spending is budgeted to rise by 3.8 per cent, slightly above the lower end of the new target range for inflation. Expenditure restraint mainly reflects continued wage moderation in the public sector, cuts in transfers and unchanged interest payments, which are assumed to be held in check by a further drop in the effective interest rate on public debt. In contrast, a sharp rise in national contributions to EU-financed investment projects would boost capital outlays by as much as 14 per cent. Overall, the 1995 budget envisages a rise in total spending by 8.8 per cent, translating into a rise both in real terms and relative to GDP.

On the revenue side, the budget calls for extra revenues, stemming from a rise in the standard VAT rate from 16 to 17 per cent, a broadening of the tax base (cuts in tax deductions for representation spending at the corporate level and a more effective taxation of fringe benefits for individuals) and reduced tax evasion. New hirings of tax inspectors as well as extended computerisation are expected to improve tax compliance. Part of the extra receipts thus generated will be used to finance revenue losses resulting from a 0.75 point cut in employers' social security contribution, the removal of the 30 per cent VAT rate on luxury items and reductions in income taxation (a tax credit for incremental investment limited to 1995 affecting 1996 tax revenues) a reduction in legal fees associated with increases in firms' own capital; and various tax incentives for small firms, employing three to 20 workers, the main source of job creation in recent years.

Under the revised convergence programme adopted in 1994, the budget deficit is scheduled to fall to 3 per cent of GDP in 1997. The latest OECD Medium-term Reference Scenario indicates that, on the assumption of unchanged policies, the general government borrowing requirement would be unlikely to fall below 3 per cent of GDP before 1999.

Progress in structural reform

A variety of measures have been taken in 1994 and are planned for 1995, maintaining the momentum of structural reform, a key element in Portugal's strategy to promote real income convergence. Its five principal objectives are:[23]

- strengthening the competitiveness of the productive sector which is dominated by small and medium-sized firms;[24]
- developing a broad and well-functioning capital market;
- rolling back the State presence in the economy via privatisation, the scope of which goes beyond companies nationalised in 1974;
- increasing efficiency in public services;
- and improving the efficiency of the labour market.

Following rapid progress over the past few years, financial market reform will be completed in 1995, putting Portuguese capital markets on par with international standards. In contrast, while restrictions affecting commercial rents are currently under review, severe restrictions continue to beset the two-tier rental housing market, keeping about 80 per cent of all rents paid below market levels and depressing maintenance spending. The process of easing regulatory restrictions is more advanced in retailing, a new law having taken effect in 1994 to facilitate the creation of new retail outlets. Given the unexpectedly rapid expansion of hypermarkets and other large stores, their Sunday opening hours were reduced to six hours in May 1995, but this is still a more liberal regime than in most other European countries.

Financial liberalisation

With respect to the *banking sector*, the authorities lowered minimum reserve requirements in November 1994, established a deposit insurance scheme in January 1995 and from August 1994 required banks to provide transparent information about lending and deposit rates. Financial margins continued to narrow, falling to an estimated 3 per cent in 1994, down from 4.5 per cent in 1990.[25] In addition, it cut by 5 points the withholding tax on *corporate bonds*, thereby ending preferential tax treatment for government bonds, while reducing from 9 to 7 per cent the stamp tax on financial transactions for enterprises. To help minimise service costs for public debt, a new market was established in June 1994, specialised in trading large allotments of *government and corporate bonds.* Financial market developments will also be assisted by policies of public debt management favouring, whenever possible, issues of fixed rate long-term debt instruments. With time, such issues may yield externalities, paving the way for the creation of a mortgage market.[26] From August 1994 non-residents issuing bonds and shares in Portugal have no longer been subject to the requirement of prior authorisation, the process of international liberalisation being consolidated by the abolition of stamp duty on the foreign-exchange operations and the removal of the withholding tax on non-residents' interest income (in June 1994). The authorities have also liberalised issues of commercial paper and the establishment of mutual funds.

The insurance sector was freed from all restrictions in mid-1994. While the number of insurance companies has doubled over the past ten years, with associated gains in market shares for small companies, concentration is still high compared with most other European countries and productivity levels are still low by European standards. Contributions to private pension funds, stimulated by tax incentives,[27] have risen sharply from low levels.

In an attempt to channel more savings towards the nascent capital market, the government also introduced tax incentives in 1995 for adherence to two saving schemes, one aimed at stimulating stock acquisitions (*Planos de Poupança em Ações*, PPA), the other aimed at attracting savings from low-income earners (*Planos Populares de Poupança*, PPP). Finally, a futures and option market is due to be opened in Oporto.

Privatisation

Development of the capital market has also been stimulated by the privatisation programme, receipts from which more than doubled in 1994, rising to Esc 188 billion, up from Esc 80 billion in 1993.[28] In contrast to previous years, a significant portion of privatisation revenues stemmed from sales of goods-producing companies (Annex Table A1). For example, one-fifth of Cimpor, one of Europe's top ten cement companies, which accounts for roughly 7 per cent of the total capitalisation of the Lisbon stock market, has been sold, with no single private shareholder owning more than one per cent of the company. Further sales of goods- and service-producing firms, including paper pulp and telecom could push privatisation proceeds to Esc 190 billion in 1995 or 1.2 per cent of GDP. The electricity power company and the second tranche of CIMPOR are sched-

41

uled for privatisation in 1996. Privatisation of other profitable enterprises, such as the tobacco – producing company, is underway. A few firms are in the process of being restructured, *e.g.* TAP, the national airline company.

Overall, a total of Esc 1 000 billion or nearly 9 per cent of GDP has been raised from sales of state-owned companies since the privatisation programme began in 1989, making Portugal the third largest privatiser in the OECD, after the United Kingdom and New Zealand. About two-thirds of overall receipts stemmed from the sale of banks and insurance companies. In the process, the state's weight in the economy has been reduced to 11 per cent of GDP from 20 per cent in 1989, while the capitalisation of the Lisbon stock exchange has increased by almost 35 per cent. In banking, public ownership has been reduced to 40 per cent, while nearly all insurance companies are now in private hands.

In the energy sector, the restructuring of the electric utility (Electricidade de Portugal, EDP) ended in 1994 with the creation of nineteen separate units, each equipped with managerial flexibility in the domain of pricing policy and invest-ment. The restructured group comprises: a production company (*Companhia Portuguesa de Produção*); a high-tension transmission company (*Rede Electricia Nacional*); four regional distribution companies; thirteen specialised service com-panies; and the holding company EDP. The four regional companies will be in charge of putting a new energy programme into effect (*Programa Energia*) aimed at raising energy investment by Esc 180 billion over the next five years. EU-funds and public sector companies would each provide one third of the investment, with the bulk of the remainder coming from the private sector. Investment would concentrate on stepping up sales of natural gas, the creation of small electricity-producing units and energy conservation. The government has already allowed private financing into the expansion of the electricity system. In 1993, the first unit of the Pego coal-fired power plant came into service, the second being scheduled to come on stream in 1995. A joint venture between Portuguese private interests and other European investors, the Pego plant could eventually provide one tenth of Portugal's electricity needs.[29]

III. Human capital development and economic convergence

Introduction

Following its accession to the European Community in 1986, Portugal significantly narrowed its income and productivity differentials relative to other EU countries. This "catching up" was largely based upon robust growth of domestic and foreign direct investment, generating a faster pace of employment creation than elsewhere in Europe. At the same time, largely thanks to structural reform, non-cyclical unemployment decreased during the 1980s, contrasting with trends observed in most other OECD countries (see Part I).[30] Over the past two years, on the other hand, real income convergence has stalled, a comparatively severe recession in 1993 having given way to a below-average recovery. The OECD Medium-Term Reference Scenario points to resumption of real income convergence from 1996 onwards, but sustaining this process will increasingly require substantial efficiency gains.

In this situation, the main forces shaping the catching-up process have come under renewed scrutiny, the role of human capital receiving particular attention. Empirical research has shown that the evolution of real per capita income in industrialised countries over the last century cannot be accounted for by increases in capital and labour alone.[31] Changes in the quality of these inputs, in addition to such factors as technical change and changes in the economic and social environment, also need to be taken into account. In recent years, "new growth" theories have emphasised externalities which flow from education, training, and research and development. In general, a well educated, trained and motivated labour force is seen to adapt more easily to new processes and new techniques, allowing productivity to rise more rapidly. The importance of these externalities may have risen over the past few decades, as firms have adopted new methods of work organisation, relying to a greater extent on maximising flexibility and on enhancing workers' contributions to firms' performance.

Over the past ten years, Portugal has made considerable progress in upgrading the quality of its human capital. Nevertheless, the education gap *vis-à-vis* most other OECD countries is still substantial. A recent comprehensive study on Portugal's comparative strengths and weaknesses found "insufficient education and training of the workforce" to be the most widely cited factor hampering firms' productivity performance.[32] In particular, a lack of intermediate managerial and technical skills was seen to stifle innovation, limit product differentiation and constrain the ability of Portuguese firms to market their goods and services abroad.

On the other hand, Portugal's relatively low level of accumulated human capital has been associated with a reliance on a labour-intensive mode of production, based on relatively low labour costs and undifferentiated products;[33] this has supported rising levels of employment and avoided the emergence of long-term unemployment at the lower end of the skill spectrum (such as has occurred in most OECD countries). Portugal will thus face the challenge of shifting industrial specialisation towards higher value-added production, while at the same time preventing a rise in unemployment for those with low and middle qualifications. Education and training policies thus need both to contribute to the convergence of Portugal's living standards with those of higher-income members of the European Union and to the enhancement of the already high flexibility of the labour market.

The basic features of Portugal's education and training system are presented in the first two sections of this chapter. These highlight the expansion and diversification of educational and training streams over the past ten years. The following two sections examine the possible effects which educational attainment may have had on the labour market as well as on the pace of real income convergence. A general assessment is provided in the final section of the chapter.

Evolution of the Portuguese educational system

Participation in general education for a majority of the youth population is a recent feature in Portugal's history as school attendance was, until the mid-1970s, either confined to primary education or to secondary courses with a narrow

Diagram 18. **STRUCTURE OF THE EDUCATION SYSTEM IN PORTUGAL**[1]

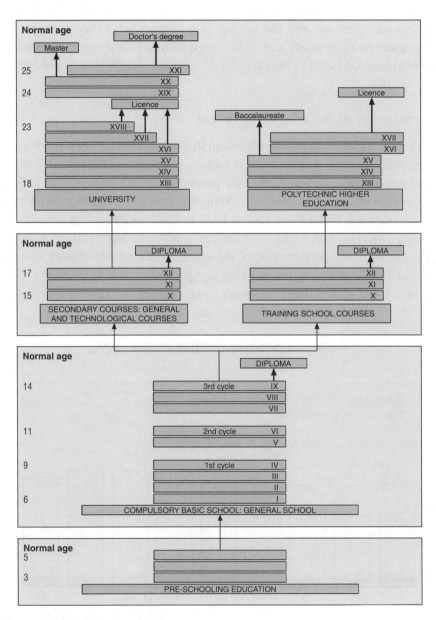

1. Roman numbers indicate years of study.
Source: OECD (1995), *Education at a Glance.*

vocational orientation. Since then, developments have been characterised by two features: first, a strong quantitative expansion, favoured by the growth of public sector education and the raising of minimum school-leaving age;[34] and second, attempts to diversify and to de-compartmentalise the educational streams, in order to respond better to the diversity of students' needs, interests and abilities (Diagram 18).

The expansion of the education system

The resources dedicated to education in Portugal have grown rapidly in the last ten years. In 1993 employment in education accounted for almost 7 per cent of total employment, almost double the proportion of ten years earlier, and close to 12 per cent of female employment. Similarly, public expenditure on education, has risen from just under 4 per cent of GDP in 1985, to above 5 per cent in 1994 (Diagram 19). The expansion of resources appears to have yielded substantial improvements in the performance of the system. Data on educational attainment show that illiteracy among the working age population fell from over a third in 1960 to 6.5 per cent in 1991, although more than 20 per cent of older persons

Diagram 19. **PUBLIC EXPENDITURE IN EDUCATION**

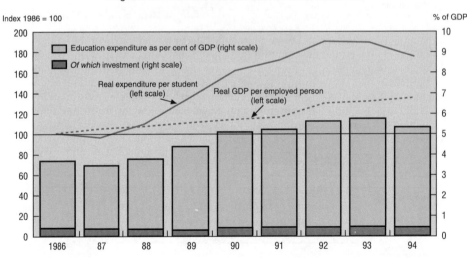

Source: New national account series. The data include EU financing on education (PRODEP).

Table 12. **Educational attainment of the working-age population, by age groups, 1960-1991**

Percentage distribution of each age group

Age group	Year	Illiterate	Literate with no educational qualification	Primary basic education[1]	Preparatory basic education[2]	Lower secondary education[3]	Upper secondary education[4]	Higher education
15-64	1960	33.9	31.5	30.4	←	3.5	→	0.8
	1970	24.6	22.6	38.7	10.1	2.0	1.4	0.6
	1981	14.6	15.3	42.5	12.3	8.6	4.5	2.3
	1991	6.5	11.6	38.2	17.6	12.2	9.9	4.0
15-24	1960	14.8	36.6	45.6	←	2.9	→	0.1
	1970	3.5	13.8	58.4	19.3	2.2	2.6	0.2
	1981	2.1	6.3	41.8	27.7	15.7	5.9	0.5
	1991	0.8	4.4	21.7	35.7	24.4	12.0	1.0
25-49	1960	35.0	30.6	29.1	←	4.2	→	1.2
	1970	24.1	25.7	37.1	7.9	2.7	1.2	1.2
	1981	10.9	15.6	50.4	7.4	7.5	5.0	3.6
	1991	2.2	9.0	46.2	14.5	10.6	11.3	6.2
50-64	1960	53.9	27.6	15.3	←	2.2	→	0.8
	1970	47.4	24.8	20.5	4.6	1.1	0.6	0.9
	1981	35.0	24.0	32.5	1.5	3.0	2.0	2.0
	1991	20.8	20.1	44.2	3.7	3.7	5.0	2.5

1. Four years of schooling.
2. Six years of schooling.
3. Nine years of schooling.
4. Twelve years of schooling.
Source: INE, Population censuses.

were still reported as illiterate (Table 12). A decline was also recorded in the proportion of the working age population leaving school without any educational qualification, while the proportion with educational qualifications increased, mainly at the lower and higher secondary level among young persons, and at the basic level among prime age and older persons. Despite this progress, however, the gap relative to other OECD countries has remained large. A significant number of youths still fail to complete basic education, and enrolment rates in secondary and higher education are well below those of other EU countries.

The gap relative to other OECD countries

Public expenditure. In 1991 public expenditure on education per student, at $2 551 in PPP terms, was only 54.3 per cent of the OECD average. This reflects both the concentration of Portuguese students at educational levels with lower unit costs (below tertiary education) and the lower expenditure per student in each educational group (Table 13). The gap in educational expenditure per student relative to the OECD average, at all levels of education, was, on the other hand, smaller than the gap in terms of per capita income, so that public expenditure in education accounted for a higher share of GDP than in the EU and OECD generally. This above-average share can be attributed to higher disbursements at the primary and secondary levels; public expenditure on higher education lagged behind that of other countries, although part of this gap is likely to be offset by the more significant presence of private schools at this level.[35] Expenditure on compensation of the teaching staff accounted for a higher proportion of public expenditure in education than in other OECD countries, with a correspondingly lower share for capital spending, at all levels except higher education. The relatively high compensation element was associated with small class sizes in the primary and secondary education sectors.

Enrolment. Data on the number of enrolled students, on a full-time equivalent basis, show that Portugal's enrolment rates in 1991 were still below those of other OECD and EU countries, and were also lower than in several other countries with comparable levels of per capita income (Table 14). While the proportion of the population of 5 to 29 years of age enrolled in primary and lower secondary education (involving nine years of schooling) was close to the OECD average, the proportion enrolled in upper secondary and higher education was considerably lower.

Early school-leaving. Despite a large rise in school attendance, and a significant reduction in both repetition and drop-out rates during the 1980s, a large proportion of the youth population still leaves formal education before completing basic education; these cohorts of early-school leavers, even when they succeed in finding employment upon entering the labour market, will lack the basic skills and knowledge necessary for further development, and are likely to find themselves at a disadvantage later on in their professional career. In 1991, according to population census data, 22 per cent of persons of 15 to 24 years of age had abandoned the school system before completing the six years of compulsory schooling. Provisional data for 1994 point to a further fall in repetition and drop-out rates, following the introduction of curricula reforms and of new assessment procedures (see below) (Table 15).

Table 13. **Indicators of public expenditure in education** [1]

	Portugal	Ireland	Spain	EU [2]	OECD [2]
Total expenditure on education					
(as a percentage of GDP)	5.5	5.5	4.5	5.3	5.2
Primary and secondary	4.2	3.7	3.2	3.6	3.5
Tertiary	0.9	1.2	0.8	1.1	1.2
Other [3]	0.3	0.6	0.4	–	0.5
Current and capital expenditure					
(as a percentage of total expenditure)					
All levels of education					
Current	94.1	95.2	88.6	93.5	91.0
Capital	5.9	4.8	11.4	6.5	9.0
Primary and secondary					
Current	95.0	96.6	89.7	94.1	90.9
Capital	5.0	3.4	10.3	5.9	9.1
Tertiary					
Current	88.4	89.5	82.1	91.3	90.5
Capital	11.6	10.5	17.9	8.7	9.5
Distribution of current expenditure					
(as a percentage of current expenditure)					
All levels of education					
Compensation of teachers	85.4	75.7	{ 66.6	{ 73.7	51.3
Compensation of other staff	3.0	8.2			14.6
Other current expenditure	11.7	16.1	33.4	26.3	31.9
Public expenditure by source of funds					
(as a percentage of total expenditure)					
Central	100.0	88.4	49.8	57.5	29.0
Regional	–	–	44.5	29.1	48.0
Local	–	0.1	5.7	11.9	–
International	–	11.5	–	1.4	–
Public expenditure per student					
(in US$) [4]					
All levels of education	2 551	2 236	2 490	3 555	4 700
Early childhood	1 506	--	1 777	2 383	2 216
Primary	2 110	1 542	1 861	2 491	2 604
Secondary	2 364	2 488	2 730	3 836	3 358
Tertiary	6 161	5 587	3 242	6 184	8 560

1. 1991.
2. Unweighted average for countries with available information.
3. Early childhood education and unclassified.
4. Converted using PPP rates.
Source: OECD (1993), *Education at a Glance.*

Table 14. **Indicators of enrolment in education**[1]

Per cent

	Portugal	Ireland	Spain	EU[2]	OECD[2]
Number of enrolled students (full-time equivalent, per cent of the population 5 to 29 years of age)					
All levels of education[3]	47.0	56.9	57.3	53.3	54.0
Primary and lower secondary education	34.0	40.7	32.0	32.8	33.6
Upper secondary education	9.1	10.3	17.0	13.0	12.3
Tertiary education	4.0	5.3	8.0	7.1	7.6
Number of enrolled students by type of attendance (per cent of population					
5 to 29 years of age)	47.0	56.9	57.3	53.3	54.0
Full-time attendance	44.4	56.1	56.7	52.0	52.1
Part-time attendance	2.6	1.5	1.2	3.1	5.5
Number of enrolled students (full-time equivalent, per cent of the population in the typical age group)[4]					
Upper secondary education	79.2	111.5	90.8	104.3	101.6
General education	..	84.8	60.7	43.9	..
Vocational education and apprenticeship	..	26.6	30.8	67.7	..
Non-university tertiary education	11.1	..	0.3	13.2	19.8
University tertiary education	8.6	..	30.9	16.4	17.5

1. 1991.
2. Unweighted average of all countries for which data are available.
3. In some cases, the data for "all levels of education" may differ from the sum of the components shown because of persons with an "undefined" level of education.
4. The typical age group is defined as spanning the typical starting age plus average duration at full-time. This ratio may exceed 100 when many of the participants are older than the reference age, and may have previously completed another upper secondary programme.
Source: OECD (1993), *Education at a Glance.*

Graduation. Comparatively low enrolment rates, together with high drop-out and repetition rates have implied low proportions finishing education on time. Available information (Annex Table A2) shows that in 1991 49 per cent of youths aged 17 (the theoretical age of graduation at the upper secondary education) had completed courses giving access to higher education. This ratio is low relative to the OECD average, although it should be noted that as late as 1985 the rate was less than 20 per cent – a substantial improvement. Moreover, within the same group only 5 per cent had completed vocational courses, while 1 per cent had attended other courses outside the normal school system, such as apprenticeship courses.

Table 15. **Incidence of repetition and drop-outs, by single year of schooling**[1]

Per cent of enrolled student

Year of schooling	1981		1990		1994[2]	
	Repetition rate	Drop-out rate	Repetition rate	Drop-out rate	Repetition rate	Drop-out rate
1	0	0	0	0	0	0
2	41	1	31	2	13	0
3	0	0	0	0	5	0
4	27	8	19	4	12	..
5	20	11	13	7	6	1
6	17	24	10	16	6	..
7	25	14	18	9	7	3
8	24	11	18	8	9	7
9	24	9	15	7	8	..
10	11	3	23	8	13	..
11	31	14	26	..	22	..
12	15	17	33	..	31	..

1. Public schools in continental Portugal. The repetition rate is measured as the proportion of students who are enrolled in the same class over two consecutive years. The drop-out rate is the proportion of students enrolled in a given year who are not enrolled in the following year.
2. Provisional.
Source: Data provided by the national authorities.

Progress in increasing graduation rates has been much slower in higher education, with only 8 per cent of those 22 years of age (the theoretical age of graduation in higher education) completing a first-degree in higher education in 1991, compared with 7 per cent in 1985. Women accounted for the majority of university graduates (62 per cent of university graduates in public university in the academic year 1989/90); overall, almost half of the university graduates are in literature, teaching colleges, and medical schools, compared to around 20 in science and engineering, and 9 per cent in management courses, a pattern which suggests little responsiveness to the needs of enterprises.

Proficiency. Survey results suggest that reading proficiency for youths aged 14 attending school has not been significantly different from that of the majority of other countries, while the distribution of Portuguese students by levels of reading proficiency has been more uniform.[36] Comparative achievement levels have been less favourable in other areas, however, especially in mathematics and science.

The reform process: challenges and appraisal

Despite the expansion of resources devoted to education, reforms were highly fragmented in the decade following the 1974 revolution, with progress hindered by political instability. An OECD review of the early 1980s recognised the enormous challenges then confronting the Portuguese educational system, recommending measures to raise compliance rates in the compulsory education sector; a strengthening of technical and vocational education at the secondary level; and decentralisation of management.[37] Addressing these concerns has been the focus of policy reforms pursued since 1986. A coherent framework for educational reform was defined by the "Basic Law on Education" of 1986, which established the general principles of educational reforms, with implementation to be phased over a ten-year period. (See Annex III for a description of main reforms in education and training policies since 1986.) The present section describes and evaluates these initiatives. The discussion is organised with reference to the Government's objectives for reform: reducing early school leaving; diversification of secondary education and curricula reform; providing for initial vocational education outside the school system; and decentralisation.

Reducing early school-leaving in compulsory education. The high proportion of youths failing to complete compulsory education in Madeira and the Azores and in the continental northern regions, suggest that socio-economic factors – such as low family income and education, and the importance of agricultural activities – may contribute to early school-leaving.[38] Other influences on early school-leaving at the compulsory level may be specific to the Portuguese education system. Factors stressed in the *OECD Review* of the early 1980s were:[39] *i)* poor teaching conditions in the first cycle of basic education in rural areas and lack of adequate pedagogical support for students with learning difficulties in isolated schools; *ii)* overcrowding and multiple shifts in schools at the second cycle associated with the expansion of the student population and inadequate school infrastructure; and *iii)* the lack of specific education streams to address the needs of those more exposed to early school leaving. The *OECD Review* also noted that the planned extension of compulsory education to nine years – unless accompanied by appropriate investment in facilities and curricula reform – could heighten the effects of factors encouraging early school leaving. It therefore called for comprehensive reforms to adapt teaching to the needs of students not destined for higher education. Recent research suggests that peda-gogical reasons may well be the dominant influence on early school-leaving.[40] The relatively low level of enrolment in early childhood education in Portugal may also be a factor contributing to the high drop-out rates in compulsory schooling.[41] Evidence from other countries suggests that early-childhood educa-tion may have a positive influence on subsequent school performance, and hence on early school-leaving.[42]

Addressing these concerns has been at the centre of subsequent educational reform. With the support of EU-funding, successive governments have favoured a strong expansion in school building, which, coupled with a reduction in the population under fourteen years of age, has significantly reduced the overcrowd-ing of schools. Also, and in parallel with developments at the secondary educa-tion level, the introduction of pre-apprenticeship and apprenticeship courses and of vocational schools may have been effective in providing alternative streams for students with learning difficulties in the first two cycles of basic education (see below). The government has introduced special programmes aimed at improving success rates among low achievers and fixed a target of 90 per cent enrolment in early childhood education to be achieved by the end of the century. However, increasing retention rates also requires that youths be convinced of the value of the qualifications provided at higher levels of education, through strengthening vocational and technical streams and reforming curricula at the secondary level.

Diversification and curricula reforms in secondary education. In the second half of the 1970s, educational reforms tended towards greater standardisation, with the abolition of professional and technical schools in lower secondary education and the establishment of a common curriculum. Measures introduced in this area since the mid-1980s have been directed at providing diversified options at the secondary and higher education level while avoiding locking students into pre-defined streams at an early stage. At the secondary level, reforms have resulted in the introduction of vocational courses in the general school system (*cursos profissionais*, and *cursos tecnicos profissionais*)[43] and of training schools (*escolas profissionais*) – autonomous schools created by local authorities, enterprises, unions and entrepreneurial associations in response to specific needs.[44] Diversification in higher education began earlier, with the introduction of polytechnic education in the late 1970s, aimed at producing high-quality technical skills.

Despite these efforts, the importance of vocational and technological streams had remained limited until the early 1990s, with only 9.8 per cent of the students in upper secondary education attending technical/vocational courses in the academic year 1991/92, and an additional 3.5 per cent attending training schools. In the case of training schools, greater local autonomy has allowed experimentation and innovation in the delivery of vocational education, but the small amount of hiring by firms through these schools points to their still marginal role within the Portuguese school system.[45] The difficulties confronting vocational education at the secondary level in Portugal are common to several other countries. A recent OECD study noted a generalised increase in the proportion of young students choosing academic rather than vocational options at the secondary level, and a tendency for vocational training to be either postponed to the post-secondary years or to be developed after entry into the labour market.[46] The challenge confronting vocational education is to enhance its status relative to academic courses and to avoid becoming too narrowly focused on problem-groups, which may stigmatise these programmes in the eyes of employers.

The limited success of the development of alternative streams has led to greater emphasis on the reform of curricula in secondary education. This educational sector has traditionally been geared to the students planning to continue on to higher education, despite the fact that only a small proportion of the student population had access to it. As a result, the vast majority of youths who did not continue on to universities would enter the labour market without any technical or vocational qualification. To correct this situation, curricula reforms at the secondary level, have introduced *cursos tecnologicos (CSPOVA)* and *cursos gerais (CSPOPE)*, targeted, respectively, at young persons who plan to enter the labour market after completion of upper secondary education and at those planning to continue to higher education.[47] The curricula reforms aim to keep school-paths open for longer, to develop curricula less focused on the provision of narrow vocational skills, and to increase the quality and relevance of the technical training they deliver. Based on preliminary information, they seem to have been successful in greatly expanding the importance of vocational education. In 1993/94, the first year in which of the curricula reforms had a generalised impact,

28 per cent of students had enrolled in technological courses, with an additional 7 per cent choosing courses in training schools.

Other reforms have taken the form of revisions to the curricula and the examination system for students in primary education. Schools have also been granted greater autonomy in the administration and organisation of instruction, with the aim of motivating each institution via an independent pedagogical project (see below). Progress with these reforms, however, has been constrained by the inadequate training of the teaching staff, which has prevented them from being fully effective as initiators and managers of the reform. Policies have recognised the importance of further progress in this area.[48]

Initial vocational training outside the school system. In addition to strengthening vocational and technical education within the school system, efforts have been directed since the mid-1980s at developing alternative avenues for entry into the labour market outside the school system. Such avenues are provided by the apprenticeship system, first introduced in 1983 and reformed in 1988, which was created in response to the needs of young people who have dropped out of the school system before completing secondary education, and who thus entered the labour market without vocational training; and by other special initial training programmes operated by the Ministry of Employment (see below). Apprenticeship courses combine vocational training provided at government centres and work experience in firms.[49] Despite a fourfold increase in the number of apprenticeships in 1993 relative to five years earlier, they represented only 2 per cent of the number of students enrolled in the second and third cycle of basic and secondary education, partly on account of their narrow conception as a programme targeted at early school-leavers. Other programmes for initial vocational training provided by the Ministry of Employment have as their objective to provide at least one year of vocational training for all persons over 15 years of age who have already left the school system.[50] Management of vocational training outside the school system is relatively decentralised.

Decentralisation of the education system. The Portuguese education system has traditionally been characterised by a high degree of centralisation, with an associated lack of adequate capacity for policy analysis, diagnostic and long-term planning and evaluation at the central level.[51] Reforms undertaken since 1986 have involved steps to transfer responsibilities from the central administration to localities, and to attribute greater powers to individual schools at all levels of administration, with their broader decision-making capabilities being defined within a statutory framework. These reforms have entailed:

- The restructuring of the Ministry of Education in 1993, with the creation of (area) departments, responsible for the conception, evaluation and co-ordination of educational policies, and of five regional education departments, with management responsibilities.
- The law on school autonomy, which introduced pilot projects in selected schools for the creation of *school councils* (with representatives of teachers, parents, students, and local and economic associations) with responsibility for the direction and organisation of courses, with day-to-day management delegated to an elected school manager.
- Broader budgetary allocations at the central level, providing greater financial autonomy for schools. In addition, schools have been granted the possibility of obtaining local financing from firms, mainly in the context of the development of programmes for technological training. This local financing, while significant at the university level, remains marginal for school at lower levels.[52]

The reforms have begun to alter the decision-making process in the Portuguese education system significantly. According to a recent survey,[53] the Portuguese system in 1991 was based on a two-level structure of decision-making, with a dominant decision-making level for central government (57 per cent of all decisions for public education at the lower secondary level), a limited role for intermediate levels of government (municipalities and Regional Education Authorities),[54] and a significant role for participants at the school level (40 per cent of all decisions) usually exercised within a legal framework determined at the central level. This pattern held, with little variation, for both primary and secondary education.[55] Decentralisation will continue with the full implementation of the reforms described above.

Assessment

Experience in other OECD countries highlights a wide variety of institutional arrangements in the decision-making process in education. Among the best-performing school systems in the OECD area are examples of both highly-centralised systems (France) and of decentralised systems (Switzerland). Decentralised systems have the potential for better adapting educational services to local needs, as shown in the Portuguese context by the experience of training schools and the apprenticeship system. On the other hand, decentralisation could also allow existing socio-economic disparities to be reinforced by the school system, unless accompanied by adequate development of educational standards, of assessment techniques, and of effective responses for dealing with failing schools and students.[56] Reforms to increase school autonomy in Portugal will thus need to be complemented by efforts to strengthen the performance of schools in disadvantaged areas.

While it is too early for a full assessment of the effectiveness of recent reforms, extending formal education will need to remain a high policy priority in the near future:

–   Increasing participation in formal education will require continued efforts to increase retention rates in compulsory education, to generalise enrolment in secondary education to age sixteen and over, and extend opportunities of access to higher education.

–   The strengthening of technical and vocational education needs to be supported by the active involvement of employers in the development of curricula and in assessment procedures, as well as through the establishment of financial links with vocational schools.

Raising enrolment rates and increasing the number of vocational streams may be mutually reinforcing to the extent that vocational programmes provide a context for learning capable of attracting and retaining students who might otherwise drop out or who are motivated by less academic approaches to learning. Thus, the value of the vocational training is not just in the occupational skills that it imparts, but also in the scope it offers to enhance general educational achievement.

The high priority attributed to education is reflected in the ambitious targets fixed for both enrolment rates at all levels of education and a more balanced blend of general and vocational streams for the year 2000. Achieving these targets will be supported by large EU disbursements over the period 1994 to 1999 under the second Community Support Framework (*Quadro Comunitario de Apoio*, QCAII) (see Box 1). Sustaining the convergence of per capita income to EU levels and reducing regional disparities are the explicit objectives of EU financial support to Portugal. The QCAII identifies the improvement in the qualification of human resources as one of the four priority areas of EU-

Box 1. Education and training in the context of the second Community Support Framework

The Second Community Support Framework (CSF), covering the period from 1994 to 1999, envisages disbursements from the EU of Esc 3 250 billion in the forms of grants, with an additional Esc 1 200 billion in loans from the European Investment Banks. Including national co-financing, the total investment effort of EU structural funds is equivalent to around 43 per cent of 1993 nominal GDP. The CSF is divided into four areas (human capital, competitiveness, social development, regional development) and eight programmes. The main features of the two programmes on human capital development are briefly described below.

Programme 1. **Basic learning and innovation**

The programme aims at improving the educational qualifications of the labour force, and at strengthening the links among education, science and technology institutions and firms. There are two sub-programmes.

–   The *education sub-programme* targets an increase in enrolment rates at all levels of education; enrolment at the secondary education level is set to increase to 90 per cent for the age group 15 to 17 years of age, with 57 per cent of secondary students in general education and 33 per cent in technical and professional schools; science diplomas are to increase to 40 per cent of all higher education diplomas by 1999, from 31 per cent in 1992; the proportion of schools with scientific laboratories is to increase. The sub-programme is predicated on seven key measures, in education infrastructure, continuous training of teaching staff, technical and vocational education, technical assistance for management and execution of these measures.

–   The *science and technology sub-programme* aims at strengthening the quality and quantity of the scientific system in Portugal, with the aim of increasing the share of R&D spending in GDP to between 1.2 and 1.5 per cent in 1999.

Programme 2. **Vocational training and employment**

The programme aims at providing all school drop-outs with a minimum one year vocational training before entering into the labour market, at improving the number and quality of medium and higher technical staff, at developing continuous training, and at favouring the integration of disadvantaged groups. It is divided into four sub-programmes.

–   *Initial qualification and school-to-work transition.* The sub-programme targets the development of the apprenticeship system and of alternative streams for youths not completing basic education. It finances the establishment of a guidance system to facilitate the transition from school to work.

(Continued on next page)

(continued)

>   – *Improvement in the level and quality of employment.* This sub-programme aims at developing vocational training programmes targeted at unemployed persons, workers in small firms and workers affected by technical change. It also assists in the development of independent entrepreneurial activities.
>   – *Support to the training and management of human resources.* The sub-programme aims at strengthening the continuous training of instructors and at developing training infrastructures, an information system on vocational training and a system of professional certification.
>   – *Training for the public administration.* The sub-programme aims at developing the training of public sector employees, to changes in technologies and in career paths.

supported programmes and devotes Esc 835 billion to measures aimed at "enhancing the basis of learning and innovation" and at strengthening "vocational training and employment".

Further education and training

In most OECD countries, the development of further education and vocational training programmes has followed the recognition that accelerating structural change is making skills and occupations obsolete at a faster pace than in the past. Moreover, decelerating entry flows into the labour market have accentuated the need for matching new demands for specific skills through retraining. The need for education and training of the adult population is particularly strong in Portugal, given the high proportion of adults with low educational qualifications. Although younger persons now account for a relatively high proportion of the total population, demographic projections point to a significant reduction in the youth labour force, ranging between 7 and 24 per cent in the ten years from 1995 according to the specific demographic assumptions used.[57]

Programmes for further education and vocational training

The Portuguese system of further education and vocational training has been characterised by the dominant role of the state, a separation between government agencies responsible for education on the one hand and training on the other, and relatively little development of training within firms. Programmes for further education and training fall in two main categories: *i)* remedial further education programmes targeted at adults who failed to obtain any school qualification, managed by the Department for Basic Education (DEB) of the Ministry of Education; and *ii)* programmes to provide vocational training and basic skills, managed by the Institute for Employment and Vocational Training (IEFP) of the Ministry of Employment and Social Security. More recently, the system has been moving towards a model combining central control over funding with a structure of provision which blends government and private agencies.

Remedial programmes for further education of adults take a variety of forms, according to the specific target population, the blend between general and vocational education, and whether they lead to qualifications equivalent to those provided by the official school system. In 1990, around 1.2 per cent of the civilian labour force was involved in these programmes. The priority attached to such programmes, targeting adults who abandoned the school system without formal qualifications, is justified by the persistently high proportion of adults in this category (9.1 per cent of persons from 25 to 65 years of age in 1991, based on population census data) and widespread adult illiteracy.[58]

The structure of the *vocational training* system was radically altered in the mid-1980s. The 1985 law, which defined the legislative framework for labour-market vocational training, strengthened the decentralisation of IEFP and introduced a tripartite body, with unions and employers' representatives responsible for overseeing the functioning of the training system. Vocational training (both initial and continuous) is provided in a variety of settings. Government programmes are delivered both directly, through *Direct Management Centres* (DMC) of the IEFP, and through *Participatory Management Centres,* operated by the IEFP, social partners and private institutes, and financed mainly from government sources (up to 95 per cent of their operating costs are covered by government finances, mainly through Community funds).[59]

EU financing has played a key role in sustaining the expansion and modernisation of training structures in Portugal. From 1986 to 1989, Social Fund disbursements for vocational training lagged appropriations, since EU directives allocating 75 per cent of structural funds for youth training projects conflicted with the Portuguese emphasis on training adult workers. The 1989 reform of EU structural funds introduced greater leeway in adapting community priorities to national needs, allowing these funds to be used in the educational area. Under the first Community Support Framework, covering the period 1989 to 1993, EU structural funds (social and regional funds) provided resources equivalent to 6.8 per cent of 1989 GDP, mainly directed at infrastructure investment in education, involving the creation of around 50 000 new classrooms, and vocational training courses covering around 1.7 million persons. Under the second Community Support Framework, the role of supporting training activities has been extended to other public bodies, while social partners and consortia of firms are allowed to benefit from direct community financing for training plans. In addition, government support may be provided to individual centres or firms.

As a result, the provision of vocational training has expanded significantly in the 1990s, with annual enrolment figures reaching 8 per cent of the labour force in 1993, up from less than 5 per cent in 1990, and public expenditure disbursements amounting to 0.7 per cent of GDP (Table 16). Most of this expansion has occurred, however, with little control over the quality of the training provided. This may have reduced the validity of training certificates as a "hallmark" of an applicant's performance, and resulted in hiring practices insuf-

Table 16. **Vocational training provided in the context of labour-market programmes**

	Number of participants [1]				Public expenditure [2]			
	1990	1991	1992	1993	1990	1991	1992	1993
Labour-market training	2.0	3.5	6.2	5.3	0.14	0.20	0.30	0.25
Training of unemployed adults and those at risk	0.1	0.1	0.2	0.2	0.01	0.02	0.05	0.04
Training of employed adults	1.9	3.4	6.0	5.1	0.13	0.18	0.25	0.21
Youth measures	2.6	2.5	2.7	2.6	0.33	0.41	0.48	0.37
Measures for unemployed and disadvantaged youth	1.8	1.3	1.1	1.0	0.17	0.19	0.19	0.09
Support for apprenticeships and related forms of general youth training	0.8	1.2	1.6	1.6	0.16	0.22	0.29	0.28
Vocational rehabilitation for the disabled	0.1	0.1	0.2	0.1	0.06	0.04	0.05	0.05
Total	4.7	6.1	9.1	8.0	0.53	0.65	0.83	0.67

1. As a per cent of the labour force.
2. As a per cent of GDP.
Source: OECD (1994), *Employment Outlook*, p. 59.

Table 17. **Labour force status of participants in vocational training programmes**[1]

	1992			1993			1994		
	Continuous vocational training	Initial vocational training	Total	Continuous vocational training	Initial vocational training	Total	Continuous vocational training	Initial vocational training	Total
Situation before the course									
Unemployment rate	..	..	14.3	5.0	24.2	13.6	9.8	34.9	22.4
Employment/population ratio	..	..	65.6	82.9	51.7	67.0	79.1	42.6	58.1
Memorandum items:[2]									
Unemployment rate	..	..	3.6	2.8	9.3	3.9	4.1	12.0	5.3
Employment/population ratio	..	..	47.8	72.3	41.0	46.5	71.7	38.0	45.7
Situation after the course									
Unemployment rate	..	..	10.9	6.3	16.5	11.4	8.4	27.7	19.0
Employment/population ratio	..	..	75.0	84.0	71.6	77.7	82.6	59.1	69.1
Memorandum items:[2]									
Unemployment rate	..	..	4.1	3.8	12.2	5.0	5.4	14.3	6.8
Employment/population ratio	..	..	46.3	71.5	41.3	45.7	70.8	38.0	45.1

1. First quarter of the year. Data refer to labour force status of course participants after completion of a training course attended nine months earlier (*i.e.* in the second quarter of the preceding year). Courses with a duration of over 100 hours in Direct and Participatory Management centres.
2. *Labour Force Survey.* Data shown refer to adults (25 to 64 years) in the first column; to young persons (15 to 24 years) in the second column; and to total in the third column.
Source: Observatório de Entradas na Vida Activa, various issues; and INE, *Inquérito Trimestral ao Emprego.*

ficiently linked to training participation, thus reducing incentives for undertaking training. Nevertheless there have been some positive effects beyond providing a buffer for firms in cyclical downturns. Nine months after the end of continuous training courses in government-sponsored centres undertaken during the second quarter of 1993, the proportion of course participants employed increased from 79 per cent, before the course, to 83 per cent after the course, while their unemployment rate fell from 9.8 per cent to 8.4 per cent (Table 17).[60] A similar improvement in labour market prospects is evident for young persons participating in initial training courses. In both cases, the decreased incidence of unemployment occurred despite a cyclical deterioration in labour market conditions. Around one-fourth of those having attended continuous training also reported an increase of their earnings. Establishment surveys in 1993 support the notion of a positive influence of vocational training on product quality and productivity.[61]

Participation in further education and training

Administrative data on enrolment in public training programmes may misstate participation rates, because they consider places and not persons, and do not cover in-firm training schemes.[62] A more accurate view of participation can be gained from labour force surveys. According to these, participation in education and training courses for employed persons was significantly lower in Portugal than the EU average in 1992[63] (Table 18). In particular, while, as in other EU countries, the incidence of education and training was relatively high among younger persons and among women, the probability of prime-age workers attending education and training courses was only two-thirds of the EU average, and only one-third for older workers.

The distribution of education and training across groups with different levels of educational attainment was also more uneven in Portugal than in other EU countries. Employed persons with upper secondary or above education were five times more likely to have received further education and training courses than less-educated workers, compared to a probability of 2 to 1 in the EU average. This confirms that inequalities of learning opportunities are reinforced throughout working life to a greater extent than elsewhere. The emphasis on remedial education programmes for adults was reflected in the greater importance of general education courses (accounting for around 42 per cent of all education

Table 18. **Incidence of education and training among employed persons**[1]

Per cent

	Portugal			European Union		
	Men	Women	Total	Men	Women	Total
By educational attainment						
Lower secondary education	2.8	3.3	3.0	6.4	7.7	6.9
Upper secondary education	14.7	11.9	16.2	10.4	17.9	11.0
Higher education	12.3	9.5	10.8	10.7	14.0	12.0
By age group						
15 to 24	12.6	14.9	13.7	27.7	28.1	27.9
25 to 44	4.8	5.1	4.9	7.0	8.0	7.4
45 to 64	0.7	0.9	0.8	2.3	3.4	2.7
Total[2]	5.0	5.8	5.3	8.6	10.4	9.3

1. 1992. Persons in employment having received education and training courses in the four weeks prior to the survey.
2. Includes persons unclassified and above 65 years of age.
Source: EUROSTAT, *Labour Force Survey,* 1992.

and training courses, compared to 7 per cent for the EU average), while the higher incidence of the more educated translated into a higher weight of courses leading to higher educational qualifications (Table 19). By contrast, the weight of vocational training courses and of training in the context of the "dual" apprenticeship system was considerably lower than in the EU average. Most of the educational and training courses were aimed at facilitating career advancement (60 per cent of all courses in Portugal, compared with 44 per cent in the EU average), while the provision of "initial vocational training" was marginal.

Training costs borne by enterprises amounted to only 2.3 per cent of total labour costs for private enterprises in 1992, only marginally higher than in 1988; of this, three fourths was for apprenticeship charges. The low provision of training by Portuguese firms may partly reflect the preponderance of small firms,[64] which have a lower propensity to invest in training; only 12 per cent of the total number of employed persons participating in vocational training courses in recent years were employed in firms with fewer than 50 employees, compared to 50 per cent for workers employed in firms with 500 employees and more.

Table 19. **Characteristics of education and training courses received by employed persons** [1]

Percentage distribution

	Portugal			European Union		
	Men	Women	Total	Men	Women	Total
Type						
General education	42.3	41.6	41.9	6.5	8.2	7.3
Higher education	38.5	37.8	38.1	20.0	21.0	20.4
Vocational training	10.2	12.3	11.3	24.7	24.5	24.6
Dual system	1.4	2.1	1.7	21.5	17.4	19.6
Other	7.6	6.2	6.9	27.3	28.1	28.0
Purpose						
Initial vocational training	4.8	7.3	6.0	26.3	25.7	26.0
Advancement in career	59.9	60.1	60.0	44.8	44.1	44.5
Changing career	18.0	16.2	17.2	9.2	9.5	9.3
Other [2]	17.2	16.4	16.8	19.7	20.7	20.2
Length						
Less than one month	34.7	40.1	37.3	27.6	27.0	27.3
From one to six months	27.6	26.9	27.2	8.2	9.2	8.7
More than six months	37.6	18.9	35.5	64.2	63.7	64.0

1. 1992.
2. Includes non responses.
Source: EUROSTAT, *Labour Force Survey*, 1992.

Assessment

Overall, these results suggest that, despite strong political commitment and a variety of initiatives introduced to improve the quantity and quality of investment in skills, the system requires further development, as it remains characterised by a relatively low participation, particularly among those most in need, and with enterprises investing little in training. Such progress as there has been towards a more decentralised delivery of training services needs to be matched by efforts to establish nationally recognised standards in skill achievement and qualifications. The traditional separation between programmes for remedial education and vocational training, under the responsibility of different ministries, may have contributed to remedial programmes taking little account of the background and occupation of participants, with vocational training focusing on too narrow a range of vocational skills. Accordingly, an agreement on training policy reached between the government and social partners in July 1991, aims at improving the integration between education and the workplace, developing training for disadvantaged groups, and involving social partners in the conception, development and execution of labour and training policies (see Box 2).

Box 2. **The 1991 Agreement on vocational training policy**

Signed between social partners and the government, in the context of the 1991 "Economic and Social Agreement" (*Acordo Economico e Social*), the agreement defines key measures and strategic objectives of vocational training policy. It covers two main areas:

Improvement of the vocational training/work interface. Given that the objective is to provide a minimum one-year vocational training to all new entrants into the labour market, the agreement commits the government to introduce: *a)* a global legislative framework on vocational training; *b)* specific measures on vocational training provided in the context of labour-market programmes; *c)* "pre-apprenticeship" courses, targeted at youths who do not complete compulsory education. It also foresees developments in assessment and recognition of competencies acquired in the dual system (through "*unidades capitalizaveis*") with active involvement of social partners; the creation of a guidance system (*Unidades de insercao na vida activa*) for the transition into working life, and of a statistical unit for monitoring results of vocational training (*Observatorio de Entradas na Vida Activa*).

Development of further education and training. With the involvement of the social partners the agreement foresees the creation of a system for recognising the competencies acquired by workers through further training, via objective validation of competencies acquired and the establishment of "official registers" of these certifications. Also, it envisages explicit recognition of competencies acquired through further training for professional advancement within firms and financial incentives for further training in the form of "grants" for workers whose job is at risk undertaking further training (the worker remaining linked with the firm, and the wage being replaced by a grant).

In addition, the agreement strengthens the involvement of the social partners in the development and management of training policy, with a commitment to the introduction of a law on employment, training and professional re-qualification. This will be aimed at assuring the adjustment of demand and supply of vocational training; the development of statistics on employment and vocational training, through a survey on the needs of vocational training in 1993-95 and studies on the impact of vocational training in different industries; and measures for the integration of disadvantaged groups, through the creation of special targeted programmes, the extension of existing programmes to the whole country, and the adjustment of existing programmes to the need of the target groups.

Education and the labour market performance of individuals

Skills acquired through formal education and training will command a premium in the labour market, which will affect individuals' incentives for investing in skills. In the short term, this premium may take the form of higher wages and lower probability of unemployment upon entry into the labour market, while, in the longer term, these may involve access to alternative career paths.

Education and earnings

Among OECD countries, workers with higher educational attainment receive higher earnings, irrespective of the characteristics of the various educational/training systems. Portugal is no exception to this pattern. A comparison of earnings data across OECD countries (Diagram 20) suggests that the relationship between education and earnings in Portugal is more pronounced than in most other countries. Earnings of men with university education, relative to those of workers with or below lower secondary education, are the highest among the countries shown, while the relative earnings of men with upper secondary education were higher than all OECD countries, except the United States. A similar pattern applies among women. Data on relative earnings by educational attainment for different age groups show a steeper profile for workers 25 to 34 years of age than among older workers, suggesting an increase of the education premium among new entrants into the labour force.

A significant positive correlation between education and earnings also obtains after controlling for the different characteristics of workers and firms.[65] Indeed, cross-country estimates of the impact on earnings of an additional year of education, after controlling for age and work experience of individuals, suggest a stronger earnings effect for Portugal (at around 10 per cent) than in many other OECD countries (Annex Diagram A1). More detailed information for Portugal in 1988, distinguishing between different types of education and controls for workers' tenure and industry of employment, suggests higher returns to schooling among employees in the private sector (an 8.4 per cent increase in earnings for one extra year of schooling) than in the public sector (5.7 per cent), with the largest increase in earnings per extra year of schooling at the level of upper secondary education (Table 20).[66]

Diagram 20. **RELATIVE EARNINGS BY EDUCATIONAL ATTAINMENT**[1]

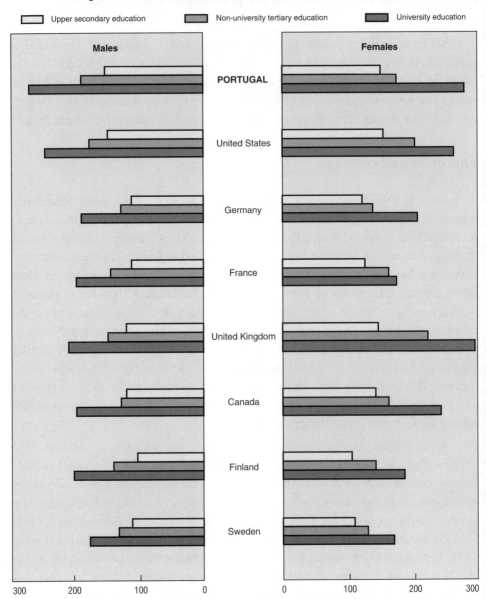

1. 1992. Relative to workers at or below lower secondary education. Data refer to persons 25-64 years of age.
Source: OECD (1995), *Education at a Glance.*

Table 20.   **Private returns from schooling**[1]

Per cent

	Public sector	Private sector
Increase in average earnings associated with an extra year of schooling[2]	5.7	8.4
Increase in average earning between different levels of educational attainment[1]		
Second cycle primary relative to first cycle primary	5.1	10.8
Third cycle primary relative to second cycle primary	4.3	7.6
Lower secondary education relative to third cycle primary education	3.2	5.2
Upper secondary education relative to lower secondary	14.7	16.2
Higher education relative to upper secondary	5.0	13.4

1.   1988. The earning increase is normalised by the increase in years of schooling between different levels of educational attainment.
2.   The estimation controls for tenure and, in the case of the private sector, average hours worked.
Source: Gepeducaçao, *O Impacto Economico da Educação sobre a Productividade da Trababho.*

A widening of the earnings distribution has occurred since 1985, with significant improvements in the premium accruing to workers with higher educational qualifications, relative to those with below basic primary education (Table 21 and Annex Diagram A2). Workers with a university degree and upper secondary education in the technical/vocational stream recorded the strongest increase in relative earnings – these also being the only two groups to experience real earnings growth since 1985 – while more modest relative gains were recorded by workers with other qualifications at or above upper secondary education. The strong improvement in the relative earnings of more educated workers was matched by similar gains for managers, technicians, highly skilled workers and foremen, while earnings of apprentices also recorded significant relative gains (Table 22). In contrast, the relative earnings position of unskilled and semi-skilled labour has deteriorated. Moreover, while earnings increase with age (a proxy for labour market experience) within each educational attainment category, a relative fall in earnings of prime-age and older workers has occurred since 1989, relative to workers between 20 and 24 years of age.[67] This increase in the relative earnings of young persons was associated with a 2 point drop in their employment share, suggesting that demographic changes associated with the passing of the baby boom may have been important.[68]

Table 21. **Recent trends in relative earnings by level of educational attainment**

Index. Average monthly earnings, relative to earnings of workers with less than basic primary education

	1985	1989	1993
Basic primary education	107.9	107.1	110.2
Basic preparatory education	117.8	109.4	110.3
Lower secondary education	157.1	152.6	152.6
Upper secondary education			
General education	173.1	166.9	173.4
Technical-professional education	182.9	204.8	220.9
Other	148.2	204.6	170.0
Higher education			
Medium course	189.9	199.6	205.8
Non-university degree	283.4	303.4	308.9
University degree	300.8	335.8	375.7

Source: Data provided by national authorities based on the administrative record of establishments, *Quadros de Pessoal.*

To the extent that workers with different levels of education are imperfect substitutes in production, changes in relative wages may be interpreted as being generated by shifts in relative supplies and demand.[69] In this respect, two general pattern have characterised recent developments in Portugal. First, a generalised shift in labour demand in favour of more educated workers is evidenced by a fall in relative earnings for workers with lower education (six or less years of schooling) occurred despite a 15 point fall in their share in employment; similarly the increase in relative earnings of workers with or above upper secondary

Table 22. **Recent trends in relative earnings by level of qualification**

Index. Average monthly earnings, relative to earnings of unskilled workers

	1985	1989	1993
Apprentices	68.1	75.8	82.9
Semi-skilled	114.5	115.2	110.3
Skilled	137.8	141.8	139.5
Highly skilled	199.5	215.7	218.8
Section foreman	196.6	211.4	212.5
Technician	270.1	296.7	306.9
Managers	354.6	402.7	431.2

Source: Data provided by national authorities based on the administrative record of establishments, *Quadros de Pessoal.*

education was associated with a 10 point increase in their employment share. Second, relative supply shifts have been significant in driving changes in relative earnings for some educational groups. Workers with lower secondary schooling experienced the largest increase in the employment share (an increase of 7 points), but suffered a sharp fall in their relative earnings. In contrast, the relatively slow growth in the supply of workers with higher education qualification (as evidenced by the rather small 1.5 point increase in their employment share) may have compounded the effect of the relative demand shifts, widening their earnings premium further.

Education and unemployment

While less-educated persons are in general exposed to a significantly higher risk of unemployment, and to a higher probability of dropping out of the labour force, the relationship between unemployment and educational attainment is weaker in Portugal (Diagram 21).[70] The unemployment rate for less educated persons was the same as for persons with upper secondary education, in contrast to the EU average where the less-educated have a significantly higher relative unemployment (Table 23, Panel A). While persons with the highest educational qualifications experienced a more significant advantage relative to the less-educated than in the EU, mainly due to relatively low unemployment among the newly qualified, younger men and older women with upper secondary education actually have a higher unemployment rate than the less educated. This pattern, of higher employment among the non-qualified than the medium-qualified, is confirmed by employment/population ratios (Table 23, Panel B). Moreover, data on long-term unemployment (spells longer than one year) by age groups and sex show a higher incidence among young men with upper secondary education, and among women with or below lower secondary education (Table 24).

The ratio of youth to adult unemployment gives some indication of the difficulties experienced by youths in their transition to working life. While, as in most other OECD countries, youth unemployment rates in Portugal are much higher than those of adults on account of their lower labour market experience,[71] this ratio has declined significantly in Portugal since the peak of 1979, reaching a level close to the OECD average for both teenagers and young adults in 1993.[72] Several factors are likely to have contributed to this favourable trend. In line with developments in other OECD countries, an easing of demographic pressures, as

Diagram 21. **UNEMPLOYMENT DIFFERENTIALS BY EDUCATIONAL ATTAINMENT LEVEL**[1]

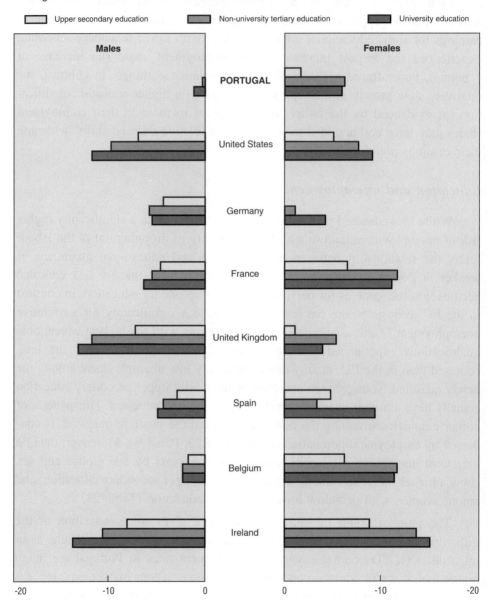

□ Upper secondary education   ▨ Non-university tertiary education   ■ University education

1. 1992. Percentage point difference relative to persons with lower secondary education. Data refer to persons 25-64 years of age.
Source: OECD (1995), *Education at a Glance.*

Table 23. Indicators of labour market performance by level of educational attainment[1]

Percentage points

	Upper secondary education			Higher education		
	Men	Women	Total	Men	Women	Total
Differentials in unemployment rates by level of educational attainment[1]						
Portugal						
15 to 24	3.7	−1.5	1.1	−0.1	−3.2	−2.6
25 to 44	−1.1	−0.8	−1.0	−0.7	−3.2	−1.8
45 to 64	−2.0	1.5	−0.9	−0.8	−2.8	−1.3
Total	−0.4	0.3	0.0	−2.3	−4.5	−3.3
European Union						
15 to 24	−7.6	−8.2	−7.7	12.1	10.2	11.2
25 to 44	−3.8	−4.1	−3.9	−5.0	−2.8	−2.1
45 to 64	−1.1	1.7	−0.1	−2.9	−5.1	−3.7
Total	−3.8	−3.2	−3.6	−1.7	−2.0	−1.8
Differentials in employment population ratios by level of educational attainment[1]						
Portugal						
15 to 24	−21.8	−12.0	−17.2	14.0	28.8	23.8
25 to 44	−0.4	15.0	8.4	5.2	15.2	9.6
45 to 64	15.7	5.5	15.5	1.5	36.3	15.1
Total	3.9	11.6	8.4	17.6	32.2	25.0
European Union						
15 to 24	12.8	17.5	14.9	−12.4	−5.1	−8.6
25 to 44	4.6	17.0	12.5	2.7	10.5	6.7
45 to 64	8.0	12.9	13.6	12.9	15.8	16.0
Total	14.5	21.9	19.9	7.5	13.9	11.1

1. 1992.
2. Relative to persons with/or below lower secondary education.
Source: EUROSTAT, *Labour Force Survey,* 1992.

reflected in a 40 per cent fall in the share of youth in the total labour force (from 27 per cent in 1979 to 16 per cent in 1993) significantly improved labour markets prospects of younger persons. An improvement in the performance of the education system, and specific programmes targeted to facilitate the school-to-work transition may also have contributed to this outcome.[73] But the improvement in the unemployment rate of younger persons in the 1981 to 1991 period also

Table 24. **Incidence of long-term unemployment by level of educational attainment**[1]

Percentage of the unemployed

	Males			Females		
	Lower secondary or below	Upper secondary	Higher education	Lower secondary or below	Upper secondary	Higher education
Portugal						
15 to 24 years	5.9	14.1	..	18.0	2.0	..
25 to 44 years	4.3	1.3	..	34.6	18.5	..
45 to 65 years	4.4	..	..	12.9	..	..
Total[2]	14.9	17.8	..	65.5	20.5	..
European Union						
15 to 24 years	7.2	4.4	7.8	7.3	5.7	9.8
25 to 44 years	16.2	12.7	16.4	20.2	14.1	19.4
45 to 65 years	6.8	6.3	4.1	5.1	3.4	1.8
Total[2]	30.3	23.4	28.4	32.6	23.2	31.1

1. 1992.
2. Includes persons above 65 years of age.
Source: EUROSTAT, *Labour Force Survey*, 1992.

embraced persons with lower attainment, suggesting that the demographic factor was the dominant influence in driving changes in relative unemployment rates (Annex Table A3).

Assessment

Available evidence suggests that the comparatively high and rising earnings differentials associated with educational attainment provide powerful earnings incentives for individuals' investment in skills. However, in Portugal's case, the impact of such incentives on school retention rates may have been muted by the importance of youth earnings to poorer families and by the low unemployment rate for less educated youths. Moreover the full potential for skill acquisition may have been impeded by tenuous links between educational institutions and firms and the absence of adequate career paths.

Convergence in per capita income and human capital

The importance of human capital for the catching up process has been documented in several studies. While, in the context of neo-classical growth models, the stock of human and physical capital is seen as affecting the steady state level of per capita income, "new-growth" theories have stressed the importance of spill-over effects associated with human and physical capital accumulation, hence their influence on the growth of total factor productivity and of per capita incomes. According to a recent survey of the determinants of productivity performance in OECD countries, it appears that one additional year of education might provide a boost to productivity levels of between 5 to 10 per cent, although the same study found little evidence of effects of education on steady-state growth rates;[74] on this account, closing the gap in average years of schooling between Portugal and other OECD countries (a gap estimated at around 2.5 years of schooling in 1985, from a level marginally above three years in 1965, according to one study quoted in this survey) might eventually raise relative productivity levels in Portugal by 13 to 26 per cent.

The gap between Portuguese per capita income and EU levels has narrowed significantly over the post-war period. This process was particularly rapid in the 1960s and early 1970s, stagnating in the following decade, and resuming after accession to the European Community in 1986 (Diagram 22). The convergence progress in per capita income was faster than in terms of labour productivity, a trend rise in participation rates and low unemployment rates boosting the employment/population ratio, in contrast to developments in other EU countries.[75] The differential in productivity levels widened in the 1970s and early 1980s, but narrowed from 1985 to 1993. A significant improvement was also recorded in terms of total factor productivity over the 1985-94 time period (Table 25).

The link between educational attainment and per capita income is brought out by Diagram 23, which plots per capita income against the proportion of the adult population (25 to 64 years of age) having completed secondary or higher education in 1991. At 7 per cent, the proportion of Portugal's population so qualified was by far the lowest among OECD countries.

Estimates of the impact of human capital on productivity at the level of the entire economy are potentially affected by a simultaneity bias, as demand for education will rise at higher income levels. Nevertheless, data for individual firms provide additional evidence of the importance of educational qualifications for productivity performance. Portuguese firms with higher (cumulative) fixed capital investment are characterised by a larger proportion of workers with higher educational attainment compared to low-investment firms, and by significantly

Diagram 22. **CONVERGENCE IN PER CAPITA INCOME AND PRODUCTIVITY**[1]

EU = 100

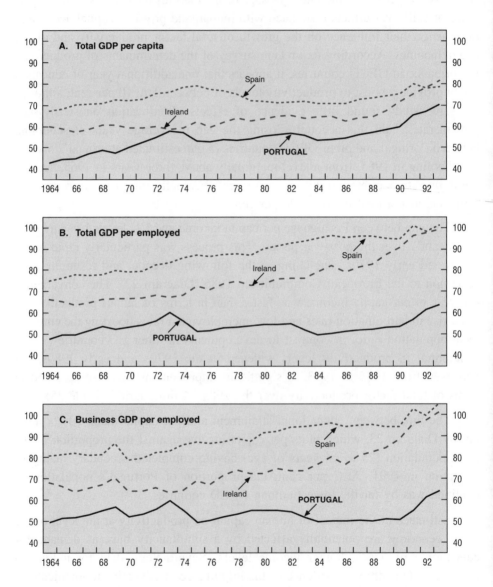

1. Values at current prices and current PPPs. For Portugal, data for the period 1986-1993 are based on new national accounts series, as provided by national authorities; data for previous years, and for business GDP, are OECD estimates.

Source: OECD, *National Accounts.*

Table 25. **Output and productivity growth in the business sector**

	1960-1973				1974-1985				1985-1994			
	Portugal	Ireland	Spain	OECD average	Portugal	Ireland	Spain	OECD average	Portugal	Ireland	Spain	OECD average
Output growth	6.9	4.4	7.3	5.2	2.3	3.7	1.6	2.7	3.3	4.7	2.9	2.6
Labour productivity	7.5	4.8	6.0	4.4	0.5	4.1	3.5	1.6	3.4	4.0	2.3	2.4
Capital productivity	-0.6	-0.9	-3.6	-0.7	-2.5	-1.8	-3.4	-1.6	1.5	2.7	-1.3	-0.5
Total factor productivity	5.0	3.6	3.2	2.9	-0.3	2.8	1.5	0.6	3.0	3.7	1.2	1.2

Source: OECD.

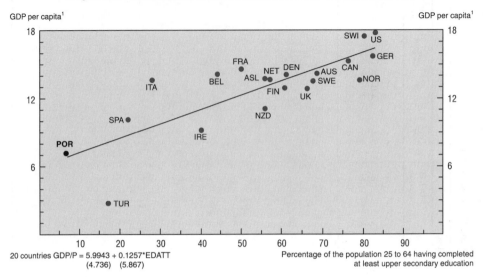

Diagram 23. **EDUCATIONAL ATTAINMENT AND GDP PER CAPITA, 1991**

GDP per capita[1]   GDP per capita[1]

20 countries GDP/P = 5.9943 + 0.1257*EDATT
             (4.736)   (5.867)

Percentage of the population 25 to 64 having completed
at least upper secondary education

1.   Thousands of US dollars, at PPP exchange rates.
Source: OECD, *Education at a Glance,* 1993.

higher labour productivity (Diagram 24). The same association between fixed investment and the structure of employment by educational attainment is evident at the level of individual industrial sectors. These data suggest that fixed and human capital are likely to be complements in the production process, jointly contributing to significantly higher productivity performance at the firm level.

Given the significant expansion in school enrolment and graduation rates in secondary education recorded since the mid-1980s, Portugal is now confronting a transition towards a more highly-educated labour force. As older and less-educated cohorts exit the labour force, the proportion with at least upper secondary education will exceed 50 per cent by the middle of the next century.[76] Productivity should thus rise as educational attainment increases. However, the effects on overall productivity of a more efficient educational and training system will ultimately depend on a broad set of influences affecting the demand and use of skills. Most important among these are the composition of industrial output, the extent to which firms can adapt their methods to use skills more extensively, and incentives for individual firms to invest in training.

Diagram 24. **STRUCTURE OF EMPLOYMENT BY EDUCATIONAL ATTAINMENT
AND LEVEL OF LABOUR PRODUCTIVITY**

Quartiles of firms with different levels of cumulative gross fixed investment, 1988

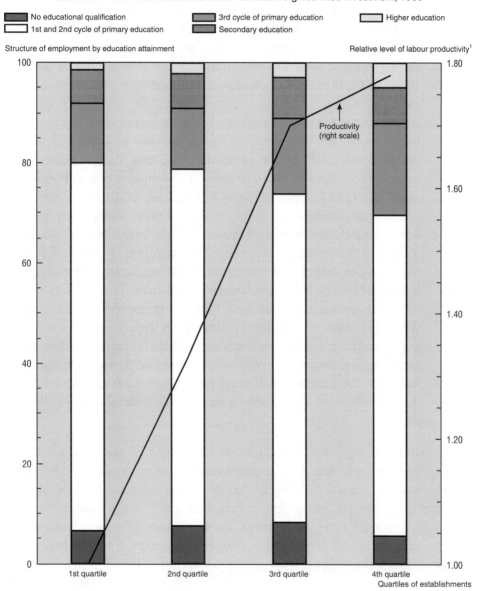

No educational qualification

1st and 2nd cycle of primary education

3rd cycle of primary education

Secondary education

Higher education

Structure of employment by education attainment

Relative level of labour productivity[1]

Productivity
(right scale)

1st quartile   2nd quartile   3rd quartile   4th quartile

Quartiles of establishments

1.   Relative to firms with lowest cumulative investment.
Source: Ministry of Education (1992).

- *The composition of industrial output.* In the Portuguese case, the dominant role of traditional industrial sectors (textiles, clothing, food processing, metal products and footwear), with a lower skill content, may have limited the demand for skilled labour through a composition effect.[77]
- *Use of skills.* Even when producing similar goods and competing on similar markets, firms can make more or less effective use of different skills. In the Portuguese context, notwithstanding recent improvements, the combination of unskilled operatives and of few highly qualified technicians and managers not only limits the contribution of workers at lower levels, but also forces those at the top to cope with simple problems on the shop-floor, neglecting long-term strategic issues.[78]
- *Incentives for firms to invest in skills.* The dominant role in Portugal of small and family-controlled firms (70 per cent of all firms) may have resulted in corporate structures and personnel management policies which limit the use of skilled labour.[79] To the extent that investment in training is more likely where firms are growing, an array of factors, impinging on corporate development, including corporate financing and the availability of long-term financing, will shape firms' efforts to provide and reward education and training. In the Portuguese context, where provision of long-term financing for family business has been traditionally limited to own funds and to bank financing, backed up by family equity, development of more sophisticated financial arrangements tailored to the needs of small firms, might allow them to move into areas that, among other things, would require more intensive use of human capital.

These influences suggest that changes in functioning of the educational and training structures will need to be complemented by changes in other dimensions in order to avoid the risk of being locked into a low-wage low-productivity trap perpetuating inadequate investment in human capital.[80] While changes in these dimensions may be expected to result from exposure to a more competitive environment, the design of tax policy, financial regulation, corporate and labour law as well as policies aimed at upgrading managerial skills will positively affect outcomes.

Foreign firms may play a pivotal role in modifying traditional attitudes towards education and training, given the significant inflow of foreign direct investment (FDI) to Portugal recorded in recent years. Comparative research on foreign direct investment has stressed the role of FDI in the diffusion of ''best practice'' technologies, and the complementarities with the stock of human capital in the host country.[81] Some foreign firms have assumed a leading role in the introduction of innovative approaches to workforce training in Portugal. In the case of AutoEuropa – the joint venture of Ford and Volkswagen for the production of mini-vans – the strategic importance attributed to the workforce skills has translated into comprehensive efforts to provide training for all employees (around 2 200 in January 1995). Training is undertaken by all new entrants, generally young workers (below 30 years of age) with a minimum of nine years of schooling, in both basic training (with emphasis on team-building and team-oriented improvements in product quality), advanced training (problem solving and quantitative methods), and simulation, vendor and on-the-job training. Training efforts are also associated with the setting up of conditions at the work place conducive to better utilisation of workers' competences, through a restructuring of work processes and organisation into small production teams that assure that the skills and competences gained are not wasted. Workers' competences will be enhanced, through periodic assessments on their performance, with training at each level of the skill ladder opening a career path to higher levels.

General assessment

Portugal has made remarkable economic progress since 1985, marked by deepening integration into the international economy, the opening-up of sheltered sectors, progress in the structural transformation of the economy and increased financial deepening. Nevertheless, convergence gains, while exceeding those of Spain, have been lower than in Ireland.

Despite improvements, Portugal's education system has, until the beginning of the 1990s, produced large numbers of people with a low level of educational attainment, offering few opportunities for effective adult education and vocational training. Several points emerge from the analysis:

  i) a large proportion of the teenage population failed to complete basic education, remaining exposed to serious risks after entry into the labour market; in addition, the system was under-performing in terms of school achievements, especially in mathematics and sciences;

ii) despite the extension of the education system, school attendance above the lower secondary education level remained below that of most other OECD countries;

iii) notwithstanding efforts to diversify streams at the secondary education level, the largest proportion of students attended courses providing general rather than vocational education. At the higher education level, the largest participation was in courses with little link to the needs of enterprises;

iv) vocational training has been traditionally marked by the dominant role of the state and little development of training within firms. Involvement of workers, firms and local communities in the conception and management of these courses was limited.

While recent reforms have significantly improved the performance of the education and training system, deficiencies persist, calling for the pace of structural reform in these areas to be maintained, if not, stepped up.

- As regards education, priority should continue to be attached to assuring full implementation of the curricula reforms and assessment procedures at the basic and secondary level, as well as to improving the management of the system – especially its efficiency and effectiveness.
- Reforms to vocational education should strengthen incentives for youths to participate in vocational courses, recognising its vital role in raising general achievement levels for students who are not motivated by purely academic instruction. The higher education system should also increase the number of places available in those areas providing skills for which demand has been rising.
- Training policies should be targeted to widen access to vocational training, both initial and continuous; to provide a broader set of competences, thus enhancing firms' capacity for internal redeployment of workers; to strengthen co-ordination through the establishment of skill and training standards; and to develop forms of programmes which specifically address the needs of small firms, *i.e.* the joint training of workers and managers.

Further progress will be facilitated by the broad consensus within the Portuguese society on the high priority attributed to developping education and training.

Such reforms will be supported by the second Community Support Framework, covering the period 1994-99, under which expenditure for education and training, including national co-financing, will reach the equivalent of 6.1 per cent of 1993 GDP.

Nevertheless, improving the supply of skilled labour will not be sufficient to attain economic convergence goals unless the demand for skilled labour simultaneously adapts. And, in this respect, Portugal faces an important challenge, having been more successful than other countries in sustaining low unemployment. A high and rising measure of labour market flexibility has enabled low-skilled labour to be easily absorbed by traditional labour-intensive industries, thanks to minimum or entry wages which are low and declining in terms of average earnings. Over time, the unemployment rate at the peak of the business cycle has declined, whereas it more than doubled in Ireland during the 1980s, where larger catch-up gains came at the expense of a deterioration in the overall labour market performance. The challenge is for Portugal to move towards a more skill-intensive industrial output to match the increasing diversity of the workforce, while sustaining its good labour market performance.

As noted above, a diversification and modernisation of the industrial structure may already be under way, as a result of deregulation, financial liberalisation and of growing foreign direct investment, attracted by comparatively low labour costs by OECD standards and the dismantling of capital controls. The faster pace of investment, technological innovation and improved industrial organisation associated with continued structural reforms in these areas, are all important for the assimilation of a higher-skilled workforce.

IV. Conclusions

Portugal's economy began to recover in 1994. Responding to the vigorous expansion of foreign markets, exports surged, helping to arrest the sharp decline in gross fixed investment. Real GDP for the year was around 1.2 per cent higher than in 1993. Even so, compared both with earlier cyclical episodes and with the economic recovery in Europe generally, the pace of economic expansion has been mild. Private consumption hardly grew, being held back by rising unemployment and falling real wages. The trade deficit narrowed by an estimated 0.6 per cent of GDP, helped by Portugal's relatively slow cyclical upturn. However, due to a steep fall in both private and official transfers, the current account is estimated to have swung back into deficit to the extent of 1.3 per cent of GDP in 1994.

Given the high degree of wage flexibility in the labour market, growing unemployment put strong downward pressure on nominal wage growth, combining with substantial gains in labour productivity to restrict the rise in unit labour costs to an estimated 3 per cent in 1994, the best result in nearly 30 years. In this setting, further progress has been made in unwinding inflation, the 12-month rate of consumer-price inflation falling to a record low of 4 per cent in December 1994, within the official target range. In a continuation of rapid inflation convergence, the differential *vis-à-vis* the EU shrank to 1 point, whereas two years earlier, prior to the 1993 recession, the inflation gap had still been nearly 5 percentage points.

The short-term outlook is for a quickening in the pace of the economic expansion in 1995 and 1996, driven by further export market growth, the coming-on stream of new export capacity and a rebound in domestic demand. A resumption of real-wage and employment gains should buttress private consumption, further strengthening gross fixed investment. Overall, real GDP growth could accelerate to around 3 per cent in 1995, which would be the best output performance in five years. A further acceleration is expected for 1996, when the unemployment rate is projected to fall to between 6 and 6½ per cent of the labour force on the basis of unchanged policies. Such a rate would still be above the level thought to be consistent with stable inflation (NAIRU), and should ensure further wage moderation, lowering inflation as well as the differential *vis-à-vis* the EU.

Monetary policy has continued to be geared to preserving exchange rate stability as a nominal anchor for wage and price setting. Following the widening of the ERM fluctuation bands in August 1993, the Bank of Portugal has kept the escudo within the previous intervention limits, but a firm monetary stance has been needed to reassert the authorities' commitment to exchange rate stability in the wake of the two parity reductions in November 1992 and May 1993. Indeed, bouts of exchange-market turbulence, largely related to the persistent volatility of international capital flows, provoked a steep rise in policy-controlled interest rates during the first half of 1994. As the authorities reaffirmed nominal exchange rate stability as the keystone of Portugal's convergence strategy, market confidence revived from June onwards, and the Bank of Portugal was able to resume its policy of cautious interest rate reductions. In the process, interest rate differentials, which had widened sharply from spring 1994, narrowed, while the escudo began to appreciate in effective terms. This upward movement in the trade-weighted exchange rate persisted after the 3.5 per cent downward adjustment of the escudo within the ERM on 6 March 1995, a move which brought the central parity into line with market rates prevailing from August 1993.

However, investors are still demanding a risk premium to hold Portuguese securities, amounting in early April 1995 to 500 basis points on 10-year government bonds *vis-à-vis* the German counterpart. Nevertheless, with economic fundamentals improving, especially with respect to inflation, continuance of the present stability-oriented policy should lead to a gradual strengthening in investors' confidence, assisting the Bank of Portugal in its efforts to lower interest rates. In this context, the credibility and consistency of Portuguese macroeconomic policy is being further helped by an increasing symmetry between interest rate requirements of exchange-rate policy and the cyclical needs of the economy. And the Bank now has, with the introduction in July 1994 of variable-rate "repos", a further means of adapting its intervention in the money market to management of the exchange rate; the rate on this instrument provides a most effective tool for steering very short-term rates while also performing a signalling function for market participants.

Currency stability should also be enhanced by a continuation of fiscal consolidation. At an estimated 5.8 per cent of GDP, the 1994 general government deficit turned out significantly better than expected. The 1.7 point decline in the deficit/GDP ratio from its 1993 level derived both from spending restraint – mainly reflecting a sharp fall in civil servants' real wages – and from revenue gains, largely based upon reduced tax evasion, notably in the domain of VAT. The latter would seem to indicate that some of the control defects noted in the previous *Survey*, with respect both to tax evasion and loopholes, have been alleviated to some extent. In the State sector, the primary balance swung back into surplus and, with the debt interest burden falling, the build-up of public debt slowed. The estimated debt/GDP ratio rose by 2.5 points to 70 per cent, compared with a jump of nearly 5 points in the previous year. The authorities have relied more heavily on external finance, pushing the external public debt to an estimated 10 per cent of GDP. Due to the steepening yield curve, greater recourse has also been made to short-term funds, shortening somewhat the average maturity of the domestic marketable debt. More active debt management has thus gone some way to offset the adverse trend in domestic bond yields.

Despite its recent improvement, the structural budget deficit is estimated to remain in the range of 4 to 5 per cent of GDP, requiring further action to correct it. This is partly recognised in the 1995 budget, which testifies to the government's continued commitment to fiscal retrenchment while improving the economy's productive capacity. On the one hand, it contains a sharp rise in capital spending, but this is offset by planned cuts in current outlays, notably a reduction in discretionary public consumption. Tax pressure is scheduled to remain broadly unchanged, revenue losses from lower employers' social security contributions and investment incentives being matched by additional receipts stemming from a rise in the standard VAT rate and a further assault on tax evasion. Hence, from a supply-side point of view the composition of the fiscal adjustment – marked by current spending cuts and a broadening of the tax base, while stimulating fixed investment – is to be commended. Yet the deficit is budgeted to remain at 5.8 per cent of GDP. Considering the better-than-expected results for 1994 and the quickening of economic activity expected for 1995, a more ambitious target should be pursued. This would provide a sounder base for in preparing the 1996 budget, in which the government will need to step up the pace of fiscal consolidation to reach its 3 per cent deficit target in 1997.

In recent years Portugal has introduced a wide range of structural reforms, extensively deregulating and liberalising the economy. Over the past twelve months initiatives have related particularly to the financial sector. Following the total liberalisation of capital flows in December 1992, reforms in this area have been aimed at eliminating tax distortions affecting foreign exchange operations and international portfolio investment in Portugal. With respect to the banking sector, the reform of the minimum reserve system has gone some way to increasing bank profitability and reducing intermediation costs which are relatively heavy in Portugal. In addition, the withholding tax on corporate bonds has been brought into alignment with that on government bonds and special tax incentives have been introduced to direct more savings from the non-bank sector towards the capital market. A futures and option market is due to be opened in Oporto in mid-1995 and steps have been taken to create a more liquid market for trading public debt. The measures taken in all of these areas have virtually completed the liberalisation of the financial sector, improving its efficiency and reducing business costs.

Financial market reform has gone hand-in-hand with privatisation, which has so far concentrated on banks and insurance companies, which have provided two-thirds of total receipts. The process has gradually been broadened to include sales of companies producing goods and non-financial services, the weight of state enterprises being reduced from 20 per cent to 11 per cent between 1989 and 1994. A further reduction to 8 per cent is scheduled for 1995-96, the privatisation proceeds earmarked for debt reduction being targeted to reach 1.2 per cent of GDP in the current year. The major industries targeted are telecommunications, paper and pulp, cement and electric power generation. Some of the other enterprises scheduled for privatisation are undergoing restructuring (*e.g.* TAP, the national airline company). For the improved efficiency of the economy it is important that the full programme be carried through.

In general, as noted in the conclusions of last year's *Survey*, progress in financial reform and privatisation should not obscure the fact that the improvement of Portugal's competitive position over the medium term demands that further action be taken to strengthen competition in other areas, notably in housing and the distribution sector. The historical freezing of rents has created a two-tier market in rental housing, depressing investment, and differences between controlled and market rents should continue to be unwound. The process of easing regulatory restrictions is more advanced in retailing, a new law having taken effect in 1994 to facilitate the creation of new retail outlets. On the other hand, Sunday opening hours for hypermarkets and other large stores, previously unrestricted, are to be limited to six hours. By European standards this is still relatively liberal, but would need to be combined with greater flexibility in the operating conditions of smaller retail outlets – control of which lies with the local authorities – if the full benefits of competition are to be achieved.

While greater competition and deregulation are essential for raising productivity and accelerating the process of real income convergence, a well-educated and trained workforce is particularly important in this regard. Over the past ten years, Portugal has seen a rapid expansion in its educational and training systems. Highlights of this process have been a sharp increase in the number of schools and teachers at all levels of education and a rise in school enrolment, especially at the basic and lower-secondary levels. As a result, illiteracy rates have dropped from high levels, while the proportion of the working age population with educational qualifications has increased significantly. At the same time, largely supported by EU programmes, the government has greatly expanded opportunities for training and retraining.

However, at the beginning of the 1990s Portugal's education and training system still produced less favourable results than those of most other EU countries. The length of effective compulsory schooling was one of the lowest among OECD countries; a comparatively large portion of the teenage population failed to complete basic education; and school attendance above the lower secondary education level remained low. At the same time, opportunities for vocational education were limited relative to need, prompting a large number of students either to opt for general education at the level of secondary schooling or to leave the school system early. Links between enterprises and the school system were tenuous, while the education systemwas excessively centralised, with an associated lack of adequate capacity for policy analysis, diagnostic evaluation and long-term planning at the central level. Given these features, Portugal's education and training systems have, until the beginning of the 1990s, turned out large numbers of people with low skills.

Aware of these deficiences, the government has stepped up the pace of implementing educational and training reform. Recent measures include the extension of compulsory schooling to nine years; the diversification of educational streams at the secondary level (including the creation of training schools); curricula reform at all levels, but mainly in secondary education, to satisfy the needs of those not aspiring to higher education; greater autonomy for schools and regional bodies, as well as a vast expansion of training opportunities outside the school system. Overall the measures already taken go in the right direction in addressing the above-mentioned deficiencies, although it is too early for a full assessment given the gradual implementation of the programme of educational reform. Additional improvements planned in the context of the second Community Support Framework are likely to maintain the momentum of further upgrading the quality of Portugal's labour force. Increasingly, attention will need to focus on the quality of the education and training provided:

- In education, the objectives should be to ensure that students complete their nine years of compulsory schooling, and to strengthen their motivation to continue their studies at the secondary and higher levels, while adapting the competencies of teachers towards those needed for the effective implementation of curricula reform.
- In the area of initial vocational training the aim should be to ensure that all youths who are currently leaving the school system early enter the labour market with adequate skills.
- For adults, attention will need to focus on strengthening firms' and workers' incentives for participating in continuous training, while taking into account the signals conveyed by the market as to the types of skills needed. This will require addressing the training needs of small firms, as well as strengthening the links between the competencies acquired through training and career advancement.

The task of ensuring that the supply of skilled labour matches demand for it is particularly important if Portugal's good labour market and productivity performance is to be maintained. Thanks to a high and rising degree of labour market flexibility, and minimum or entry wages which are low in terms of average earnings, Portugal's labour market has been insulated from the high structural unemployment rates afflicting many other countries in Europe. The challenge is to create the conditions where the demand for industrial skills matches the output of the education and training system. As the main text indicates, this would tend to occur where capital investment is increasing, skill-management at the firm level improving and the conditions in place for small firms to develop and expand.

The educational policies that have been put into place should yield dividends in terms of a rapidly rising supply of educated and skilled labour. Provided such policies continue to be complemented by other elements of structural policies, aimed at facilitating the growth of the business sector, they should lead to higher real incomes thanks to augmented levels of labour productivity. Regulatory reform, privatisation and fiscal convergence are all essential to this process, and if carried through should enlarge the scope for non-inflationary growth, thereby speeding up the process of real income convergence.

Notes

1. New employment data (1992), based upon a larger sample used in the employment survey, revealed larger numbers of self-employed people than estimated earlier. In addition, a new index of industrial production came into use in 1993, covering a wider range of activities. Following the completion of the Single European Market, a new system of foreign trade statistics was established in 1993 in line with the requirements of INTRASTAT, the new information-gathering system for the EU, as well as a new balance-of-payments methodology. The introduction of INTRASTAT has made it difficult to compare Portugal's trade flows in 1993 with those in previous years, which were based upon customs records, as in other countries.

2. The new national accounts are based upon the population census of 1981. The new census of 1991 revealed a population figure which was about half a million lower than estimated on the basis of previous census data.

3. F. Klau and Mittelstädt A. (1986), "Labour market flexibility", *OECD Economic Studies*, No. 6, pp. 14-27.

4. See: OECD (1994), *Economic Survey of Portugal*, pp. 17-18.

5. The unemployment insurance replacement ratio stood at 32.5 per cent in 1993. The minimum wage in the non-agricultural sector has fallen from 45.6 per cent of average earnings in 1989 to 41.5 per cent in 1993.

6. D. Grubb and Wells W. (1994),"Employment regulation and patterns of work in EU countries", *OECD Economic Studies*, No. 21.

7. In 1989 and 1991, firing restrictions were eased through a wider range of admissible lay-off motivations, the possibility of collective dismissals and easier resolution of severance pay disagreements.

8. Permanent work contracts account for nearly nine-tenths of all contractual relationships. A work contract becomes automatically "permanent" after three years of employment or a maximum of two renewals.

9. See: OECD (1992), *Economic Survey of Portugal*, pp. 100-101.

10. In October 1990, Portugal abandoned its 13-year old policy of small pre-announced devaluations of the exchange rate. The nominal effective exchange rate began to rise. Participating in the Exchange Rate Mechanism since April 1992, the escudo was devalued in November 1992, in May 1993 and in March 1995.

11. Tradeables exclude services and construction and account for 47.5 per cent of the basket for consumer goods and services.

12. OECD (1995), *Economic Survey of Italy*, pp. 16-24.

13. Bank of Portugal (1994), *Quarterly Bulletin*, June 1994, pp.49-56.

14. Monitor Company (1994), *Construir as vantagens competitivas de Portugal*, Lisbon, p. 80.

15. AutoEuropa, a joint venture by Ford and Volkswagen with investment outlays equal to Esc 450 billion or 2.9 per cent of GDP, began production of multi-purpose mini-vans at a plant in Palmela in 1995. Output from this plant has originally been forecast to account for more than 10 per cent of total exports.

16. "In the context, the Banco de Portugal sought whenever possible to ease official interest rates down, while maintaining an assiduous presence in the foreign exchange market in defence of the escudo ..." Bank of Portugal (1994), *op. cit.*, p. 10.

17. Foreign exchange deposits, *i.e.* deposits denominated in foreign currency and held in Portugal, accounted for 3 per cent of the L-aggregate in 1994.

18. The figures are based on revised national accounts data. See Part I.

19. A sharp rise in tax audits combined with a new code of sanctions (January 1994), making tax evasion a crime punishable by imprisonment, strengthened the efficiency of tax collection.

20. Conditions for the release of EU transfers have been tightened, ruling out "bridging" credits and making payment conditional upon the attainment of budget deficit targets as delineated in convergence plans.

21. Following a change in the privatisation law, proceeds earmarked for debt by-back must now account for at least 40 per cent, compared with a mandatory 80 per cent under the previous law.

22. In 1993, the rating of Portugal's long-term external debt was upgraded to AA– by the agency Standard & Poor's. The short-term debt, rated for the first time, received the maximum rating.

23. Ministério das Finanças (1994), *Relatório do Orçamento do Estado para 1995*, pp. 91-102.

24. For a detailed review of structural reform, see OECD (1994), *Economic Survey of Portugal*, pp. 48-76.

25. Traditional intermediation activity still accounts for at least 75 per cent of banks' value added.

26. Ministério das Finanças (1994), *Relatorio do Orçamento do Estado para 1995*, p. 96.

27. Subject to a ceiling, employers' and employees' contributions to private pension funds are tax-deductible.

28. From 1993, proceeds for debt buy-back must account for at least 40 per cent, compared with a mandatory 80 per cent under the privatisation law of 1989. The split between receipts earmarked for debt redemption and restructuring of ailing public companies is decided by the government, with no need for parliamentary approval.

29. OECD (1994), *Economic Survey of Portugal*, pp. 68-69.

30. For an evaluation of structural reforms see OECD (1994), *Economic Survey of Portugal*, pp. 48-76.

31. For a discussion of these issues see OECD (1994), *The OECD Jobs Study*, Part II, pp. 113-116.

32. Monitor (1994), *Construir as Vantagens Competitivas de Portugal*, p. 58.

33. Portugal's labour costs in manufacturing in 1993 (as measured by hourly compensation costs for production workers in US dollars) were around one-quarter of OECD and EU levels, and marginally lower than in the Asian NIEs. See BLS (1994), ''International Comparisons of hourly compensation costs for production workers in manufacturing 1975-93'', *Report 887*, p. 6.

34. Compulsory education has been progressively increased from four years of schooling (extended to women in 1960), to six years in 1964 (involving education until age of 12) and to nine years (up to age 14) for the cohort entering school in 1987.

35. Among full-time students, a relatively high proportion (10 per cent) attend private education (see Table 14 below). The role of private schools is most significant at the university level, which recorded a large expansion in recent years, mainly on account of supply constraints (including the existence of fixed admission limits) in public universities.

36. These results are presented and discussed in OECD (1993), *Education at a Glance*, pp. 151-171.

37. OECD (1984), *OECD Review of National Educational Policies for Portugal*, p. 19.

38. Survey data on youths who left school before the age of 15 in the northern region show that early school-leaving is more important in larger households with lower incomes, and that the age of the school-leaver is lower in the case of parents with lower educational attainment. While only 9 per cent of these early school-leavers were not in employment upon exiting school, around one-quarter were employed as unpaid family workers and, in several cases, in the same industry of employment as their fathers. See Azeredo J. (1995), ''Estudo sobre as condições de Inserçao Precoce de Jovens no Mercado de Trabalho na Região do Norte'', mimeo, Universidade Católica Portuguesa, January, pp. 11-31.

39. OECD (1984), *Review of National Educational Policies for Portugal*, pp. 26-28.

40. According to the survey referred to above, the majority of parents of drop-out youths reported ''incompatibility between students and schools'' as the dominant reason for early school-leaving. See Azevedo (1995) *op. cit.*, p. 10.

41. The average duration of early childhood education in Portugal, at 1.35 years, was lower in 1991 than in most other EU countries. See OECD (1993), *Education at a Glance*, p. 114.

42. See OECD (1994), *The OECD Job Study*, p. 134.

43. *Cursos profissionais* at the lower secondary levels, introduced in 1983, combine one-year courses and a six month traineeship, and award training certificates that allow integration into professional careers; *cursos técnicos profissionais* at the secondary level, introduced with pilot experiences in 1983 and reformed in 1989, combine general, specific and technical education with work experience in the context of three-year courses, leading to an EU level 3 qualification and guaranteeing access to higher education.

44. *Training schools,* introduced in 1989, are directed to persons completing the second and third cycle of basic education; they currently offer three-year courses, as well as traineeships

within enterprises after completion, leading to the award of EU level 2 and level 3 certifications.

45. A recent audit by Coopers & Lybrand of the experience of Portuguese training schools (*Insercao Profissional dos Primeiros Diplomados pelas Escolas Profissionais*, July 1994) noted, among the weakness of the current system, the difficulties in strengthening the involvement of firms and social partners in their management, weak recruitment links with firms (15 per cent of training schools' students were unemployed after graduating), as well as a concentration of training schools in medium and large urban areas.

46. See OECD (1994), *Vocational Education and Training for Youth: Towards Coherent Policy and Practice*, pp. 9-11.

47. All secondary schools will offer the two streams, with both streams combining an area of general education, one of technical education, and one of scientific and artistic education, with different blends of courses and of hours in each area according to the chosen streams. CSPOPE are organised in four groups (scientific; arts; economic and social sciences; and human sciences), while CSOPVA offer eleven courses (computer sciences; civil construction; electronics; mechanics; chemicals; design; arts; administration; commercial services; communications; social animation) organised within four groups. The two streams will provide identical qualifications, and will both provide eligibility for access to higher education.

48. With the implementation of the programme FOCO, teacher training is expected to reach more than a third of all teaching staff in the year 1994/95, with public expenditure worth Esc 10.3 billion.

49. The "dual" apprenticeship system is structured in three forms: *i)* "pre-apprenticeship" courses for people 14 to 24 years of age who have only completed the first cycle of basic education; *ii)* two/three year apprenticeship courses for people with six years of education, leading to diplomas equivalent to the third cycle of basic education; *iii)* apprenticeship courses of three/four years duration for persons who have completed the third cycle of basic education (nine years of schooling), awarding diplomas equivalent to secondary education.

50. In addition to vocational and training provided through labour-market programmes managed by the Ministry of Employment, specific vocational courses for youths are provided by various Ministries, such as the Ministry of Health (through *Health Service Technical Colleges*, and *Nursing Colleges*), the Ministry of Trade and Tourism (through the *National Institute of Tourism Training*), the Ministry of Industry (through the *National Engineering and Industrial Technology Laboratory*), and the Ministry of Agriculture.

51. See OECD (1984), *op. cit.*, p. 21. This is also highlighted by the comparatively poor quality of educational statistics.

52. Data on public expenditure in education in 1991 highlighted the dominant role of central government as only source of public expenditure in education, which compares with a significant role for spending at the local and regional level in other OECD countries.

53. The survey relating to the year 1990/91 covers private and public education at the primary and secondary level, and decisions in four areas: *i)* the organisation of instruction; *ii)* planning and structure of courses; *iii)* personnel management; and *iv)* allocation and use of resources. Experts are questioned on different decisions, and results are aggregated attribut-

ing equal weight to each area, and to each individual decisions within each area. Aggregate results using different weighting scheme, discussed in OECD (1995), *Decision Making Processes in Education Systems of 14 OECD Countries*, produce results which are similar to those presented in the text.

54. Since 1976, Madeira and Azores have been granted significant autonomy, extending to educational and training systems, whose structures and facilities are managed by the respective regional bodies.

55. Schools were reported as being the dominant decision-making level in the area of instruction, where they were responsible for accepting students' enrolment, streaming and grouping of students, teaching methods and choice of textbook, assistance to pupils, and methods of assessment; and in personnel management , where they were responsible for the terms of service of all staff, and for hiring and firing of heads of schools. Schools played, however, a limited role in the area of planning and structuring of education, for example in designing school programmes (choice of range of programmes and subject matters, syllabus, and the creation or abolition of grades), and in the area of the allocation and use of resources within the school (with partial responsibility only in investment and operating expenditures).

56. OECD (1994), *Economic Survey of the United States*, pp. 91-94.

57. See OECD *Employment Outlook* 1994, p. 75.

58. Data based on completed education are likely to underestimate significantly the size of the deprived population. Recent research has argued in favour of a broader concept of "functional illiteracy", encompassing communication, interpretative and numeric skills, and emphasising the need of assessment in specific functional contexts (such as the workplace). The "Literacy Assessment Survey" for Canada in 1989, which applied this broader concept, indicated that "roughly one in eight adults with more (than nine) years of schooling could be classified as a "false literate". See OECD (1992), *Adult Illiteracy and Economic Performance*, pp. 16-18.

59. *Direct Management Centres* are managed directly by the IEFP; 22 centres were in operation in 1993, with training activities reaching almost 20 000 persons, offering courses of different lengths. *Participatory Management Centres* are set-up as a result of agreements between the IEFP and sectoral and regional organisations, with government support in management and financing; 23 such centres were operating in 1993, with participation of 34 000 trainees, and providing courses mainly of short duration.

60. Data cover only a small fraction of all course participants (those who attended courses longer than 100 hours) in Direct and Participatory Management Centres.

61. The proportion of firms recording an increase in productivity in the 1991-93 period is higher for those with training programmes (73 per cent) than for other enterprises (39 per cent); the same finding applies to product quality. See Ministério do Emprego e da Segurança Social, "Impacto nas empresas da Formação Profissional, Periodo 1991-1993", mimeo.

62. Such data are based on attendance, irrespective of the length of the course.

63. The data, from the European Community Labour Force survey, refer to participation to education and training in schools, training centres and within firms during a specific period of 1992 (the four weeks prior to the reference week of the survey).

64. In 1991, 59.5 per cent of Portuguese employment in industry and market services was in enterprises with less than 100 employees, 19.5 per cent in enterprises with between 100 and 499 employees, and 21 per cent in enterprises with more than 500 employees. The share of employment in small enterprises was higher than in most other EU countries, although lower than in Italy and Spain, and increased in the period from 1988 to 1991. See OECD (1994), *Employment Outlook*, p. 124.

65. Earnings data are based on an administrative record of establishments (*Quadros de Pessoal*), excluding agriculture and public administration.

66. Similar estimates of the impact of years of schooling on earnings (at around 10 per cent) are reported in Kiker and Santos (1991), *Human Capital and Earnings in Portugal*, Economics of Education Review, pp. 187-203. These estimates, based on data for 1985, control for a larger set of individual and industry variables, such as size of firm, location, industry, and skill requirement of jobs. In addition, the authors estimate the impact on earnings of years of job-tenure, which is interpreted as a proxy for firm-specific training, at 2.6 per cent; the impact of years of work-experience in other firms, which is interpreted as a proxy for general training, is of 1.3 per cent.

67. This is true for most educational categories, the only exceptions being for individuals with an upper-secondary technical education or non-university higher education.

68. OECD (1993), *Employment Outlook*, pp. 168-170, in noting a generalised deterioration in relative earnings of young people over the five years to 1987, stressed the close association between the onset of the baby-boom and changes in earnings differentials; in Portugal, the peak in the number of young people came earlier than in other European countries.

69. See Katz, Lawrence F. and Kevin M. Murphy (1992), ''Changes in relative wages, 1963-1987: Supply and Demand Factors'', *Quarterly Journal of Economics*, February, pp. 35-78, for an analysis applied to the United States.

70. In Ireland, for example, the differential between the unemployment rate for those with low and high level of educational qualification is extremely marked. See OECD, *Economic Survey of Ireland*, 1995.

71. Data on relative unemployment rates by level of educational attainment and age, reported in *The OECD Jobs Study*, pp. 120-121, suggest that, in Portugal, the advantage provided by higher education increases with age up to age 35 to 44 and decreases thereafter, a pattern contrasting with the steady decline of most other OECD countries. This suggests that a lack of labour market experience tends to dampen the advantage provided by more education in the earliest years of working life.

72. See OECD, *Employment Outlook 1994*, p. 22. The increase of these ratios in 1994 reflect the higher cyclical sensitivity of youth unemployment during recessions.

73. In addition, an increases in school retention rates, as measured in labour force surveys, will mechanically lead to lower youth unemployment, as the unemployment rate of Portuguese students is only half that for other youths; see OECD, *Employment Outlook 1988*, p. 60.

74. See Englander and Gurney (1994), ''Medium Term Determinants of OECD Productivity'', OECD *Economic Studies 22*.

75. The gap relative to the EU level is larger when assessed in term of hourly labour productivity, on account of both an above-average number of hours worked by full-time workers in Portugal, and of below-average weight of part-time employment; see European Commission (1993), *Employment in Europe*, pp. 81-88. Estimates of annual hours worked are based on "normal hours", as measured in the Community Labour Force Survey.

76. Based on graduation rates in 1991. Achievement of the targets for enrolment in secondary education set in the second Community Support Framework would imply much higher educational attainment levels.

77. Changes over the last decade appear to have further reinforced these traditional sectors. See Banco de Portugal (1994), *Report of the Directors and Economic and Financial Survey for the year 1993*, pp. 23-27.

78. Monitor (1994), *Construir As Vantagens Competitivas de Portugal*, p. 58.

79. Demand for more educated workers may also have been constrained by a prevalence of low-educational attainment among employers; at 22 per cent in 1991, the proportion of employers with upper secondary and higher educational attainment was lower than among employees (24 per cent).

80. Snower D. (1994), "The Low-skill, Bad-Job Trap", *IMF Working Papers*, characterises a "low-skill, bad-job trap" as one where workers acquire insufficient training and firms provide insufficient skilled vacancies, on account of externalities in the vacancy and in the training-supply functions. In this model, firms will have little incentive to provide good jobs, and workers have little incentive to acquire skills, even in the presence of high and rising earnings differentials.

81. Eduardo Borensztein, José De Gregorio and Jong-Wha Lee (1994), *How Does Foreign Direct Investment Affect Economic Growth?*, pp. 8-16.

Annex I

Major privatisations

Table A1. **Major privatisations, 1989-1994**

Enterprise	Date	Percentage sold	Method	Total revenue (in million escudos)	Sector
Banco Totta and Açores (first tranche)	10.07.89	49.0	Public offer	285 794	Banking
Tranquilidade (first tranche)	04.12.89	49.0	Public offer	257 775	Insurance
BTA (second tranche)	31.07.90	31.0	Public offer	223 552	Banking
Centralcer	12.11.90	100.0	Public offer	345 851	Food/beverages
Banco Português Atlantico (first tranche)	11.12.90	33.0	Public offer	497 527	Banking
Banco Espiritu Santo (first tranche)	09.07.91	40.0	Public offer	608 661	Banking
Banco Fonsecu Burnay	27.08.91	80.0	Public tender	360 800	Banking
Banco Espiritu Santo (second tranche)	25.02.92	60.0	Public offer	890 176	Banking
Banco Português Atlantico (second tranche)	25.05.92	17.6	Public offer	506 250	Banking
Petrogal	04.06.92	25.0	Public tender	408 000	Oil
Imperio	17.11.92	100.0	Public offer	255 122	Insurance
CPP	02.12.92	100.0	Public offer	408 241	Banking
União Bancos Portguês	03.02.93	61.1	Public offer	244 194	Banking
Banco Português Atlantico (third tranche)	07.07.93	17.5	Public offer	323 748	Banking
Banco Português Atlantico (fourth tranche)	25.03.94	7.5	Public offer	153 750	Banking
SECIL	31.05.94	51.0	Public offer	311 875	Cement
CMP	31.05.94	80.0	Public offer	318 223	Cement
CIMPOR	04.07.94	20.0	Public offer	396 100	Cement
BPSM	16.11.94	80.0	Public offer	372 832	Banking

Source: Data supplied by the Portuguese authorities.

Annex II

Supporting material to Part III

Table A2. Educational attainment

Number of persons attaining certain educational qualifications as a percentage of the relevant age group

	Upper secondary education													First degree from higher education			
	a) Diploma giving access to higher education									b) Other[1]			Typical graduation age	Total			Typical graduation age
	Total			General			Technical or vocational										
	1985	1990	1991	1985	1990	1991	1985	1990	1991	1985	1990	1991		1985	1990	1991	
Portugal	**19**	**41**	**49**	**19**	**36**	**44**	..	**4**	**5**	..	..	**1**	**17**	**7**	**6**	**8**	**22**
Australia	..	41	41	..	14	13	..	27	28	..	46	46	18	..	21	24	21
Austria	..	69	..	15	33	..	..	36	..	..	46	46	17	7	8	8	22
Belgium	72	72	73	72	72	73	..	36	..	..	..	..	17	13	17	13	22
Canada	88	82	86	30	33	32	57	49	54	..	..	..	19	22	32	33	22
Denmark	43	45	46	43	45	46	57	49	54	..	..	..	18	10	15	17	22
Finland	60	67	70	20	28	31	..	..	..	76	18	14	19	15	17	17	23
France	21	25	24	21	25	24	39	39	40	5	70	73	18	12	15	16	21
Germany	..	80	..	..	54	..	..	..	..	87	6	6	18	13	13	13	25
Greece	68	77	81	68	70	74	..	26	..	..	102	93	17	..	12	13	21
Ireland	39	46	51	16	17	18	24	7	7	..	1	1	17	14	17	17	21
Italy	..	..	..	..	..	..	..	29	33	..	12	13	18	8	9	10	22
Japan	..	91	91	66	66	67	25	25	25	..	20	22	17	..	22	24	22
Netherlands	54	57	60	29	29	29	25	28	31	16	31	31	18	6	8	8	21
New Zealand	16	31	35	16	31	35	..	..	..	..	17	18	17	14	15	16	23
Norway	57	63	71	36	35	39	21	28	32	..	..	..	18	19	27	31	21
Spain	52	63	64	26	33	34	26	29	30	..	..	..	18	14	19	20	23
Sweden	79	79	80	21	19	20	59	60	61	68	71	..	18	16	12	13	25
Switzerland	17	17	17	17	17	17	..	11	16	68	71	70	19	7	8	8	23
United Kingdom	..	45	50	..	34	35	..	11	16	..	71	70	17	..	17	18	21
United States	76	74	75	76	74	75	..	..	..	..	46	44	17	23	29	29	22

1. Some of these courses are often completed by persons who also obtain diplomas of type a). The sum of a) and b) may, therefore, exceed 100 per cent.

Source: OECD (1994), The OECD Jobs Study, p. 141.

Table A3. **Trends in unemployment rates by age groups, sex and level of educational attainment**

Percentage points

	Males					Females				
	Primary education	Lower secondary education	Upper secondary education	Higher education	Total	Primary education	Lower secondary education	Upper secondary education	Higher education	Total
15 to 24										
1981	9	15	14	7	10	24	32	25	5	25
1991	6	14	17	9	8	11	21	19	7	13
25 to 34										
1981	3	3	3	2	3	9	7	7	2	7
1991	4	3	4	2	4	11	10	8	3	9
35 to 44										
1981	2	1	1	–	2	6	3	3	1	5
1991	3	2	2	1	3	9	6	4	1	7
45 to 54										
1981	2	2	2	–	2	5	3	3	1	4
1991	3	2	2	1	3	7	5	4	1	7
55 to 64										
1981	2	2	2	1	2	3	3	2	1	–
1991	4	5	4	3	4	6	7	6	2	6
Total										
1981	4	6	5	1	4	11	15	13	2	11
1991	4	6	5	2	4	9	12	9	2	9

Source: INE, Population Censuses.

Diagram A1. **THE IMPACT OF EDUCATION ON EARNINGS**[1]

Percentage increase in earnings from one extra year of education, 1987

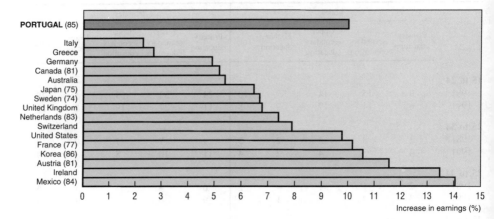

1. The estimates are based on regressions which control for an individual's age and work experience.
Source: Psacharopoulos G. (1992), *Returns to investment in education: a global update,* The World Bank, Policy Research Working Papers, pp. 42-43.

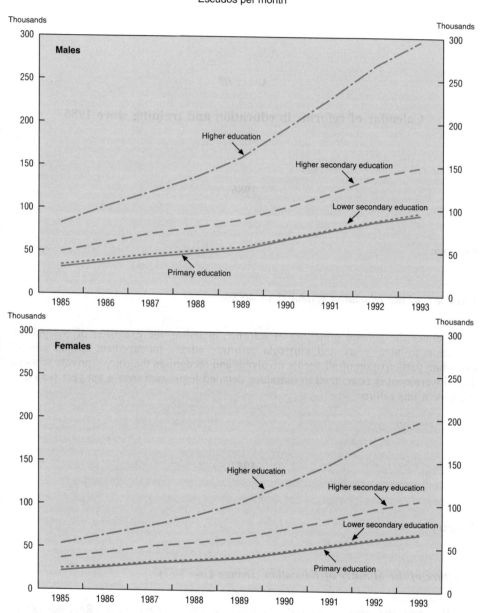

Diagram A2. **EARNINGS BY LEVEL OF EDUCATION ATTAINMENT**

Escudos per month

Source: Quadros de Pessoal.

105

Annex III

Calendar of reforms in education and training since 1986

1986

October

Basic law of the education system (Law 46/86)

Defines the general principles of reforms, including the extension of compulsory education to nine years and curricula reforms; adapts management to the aim of extending participation of all agents involved; and recognises the role of private schools. The Government is committed to introduce detailed legislation over a ten year period to implement this reform.

1987

January

Structure of the Ministry of Education (Decree Law 3/87)

Redefines the organisation of the Ministry of Education and creates Regional Directorates, who are responsible for co-ordination and support of schools in basic and secondary education and for the management of their financial and human resources.

1988

September

Law granting autonomy to universities (Law 108/88)

Grants autonomy to universities in statutes, scientific-and pedagogic projects, personnel and administrative management; the central government remains financially responsible for assuring their functioning.

November

Dual apprenticeship system (Decree Law 436/88)

Reforms the apprenticeship system, to strengthen its administrative structure, modify the grants for apprenticeships and improve the integration of general education courses within curricula. Establishes a tripartite structure, with responsibility for development and assessment of the system, while assigning responsibility for detailed implementation to the Ministry of Labour.

1989

January

Creation of training schools (Decree Law 26/89)

Introduces training schools, created by public and private bodies following protocols with the state; endowed with pedagogic, administrative and financial autonomy, these colleges educate persons bound for entry into the labour market, although not precluding access to higher education.

February

Autonomy of schools (Decree Law 43/89)

Establishes the autonomy of schools, at the primary and secondary levels, for the management of curricula and complementary pedagogical activities, for the orientation and streaming of students, for the continuous training of staff, for financial and administrative management; establishes the gradual transfer of these competencies.

August

Basic principles of curricula reform (Decree Law 286/89)

Lays out the general principles of curricula reform at the basic and secondary level, including the creation of a school-specific section of the curricula, the reform of the testing and evaluation systems, and the strengthening of pedagogical measures for support of students with learning needs; the new curricula are introduced in 1989/90 for the first year of basic education, and progressively generalised thereafter.

October

Framework law on training of teachers (Decree Law 344/89)

Defines the general principles for the training of teachers at the pre-primary, primary and secondary level, in terms of both initial training and continuous training; the latter may be provided on the initiative of individual schools, regional and central government bodies, with attendance linked to career progression.

1991

May

School direction and management, primary and secondary education (Decree Law 172/91)

Introduces new governing bodies for schools at the pre-primary, primary and secondary levels; sets up school-councils, with representatives of teaching and non-teaching staff, parents, students, local government bodies and social partners, with responsibilities for school direction, while management is delegated to an executive director. The new governing bodies will be introduced gradually.

October

Introduction of pre-apprenticeship courses (Decree Law 383/91)

Defines general principles for pre-apprenticeshup courses.

Framework law on vocational training (Decree Law 401/91, and Decree Law 405/91)

Defines the general principles of vocational training provided by both school and labour market programmes. Vocational training, encompassing technical, scientific and general training, may be provided by private and public entities, with the government retaining financial responsibility for training of youths, unemployed and disadvantaged groups, and with firms responsible for the continuous training of the employed. Conditions will be created to generalise access to initial and continuous training.

1992

April

Information system on labour-market vocational training (Decree Law 59/92)

Establishes an information system measuring vocational training activities and outcomes.

May

Certification of vocational training (Decree Law 95/92)

Establishes a system for the certification of labour-market vocational training.

November

Training of teachers (Decree Law 249/92)

Establishes the legal and administrative framework for the continuous training of teachers.

1993

April

Structure of the Ministry of Education (Decree Law 133/93)

Redefines the competences of the Ministry Education and re-structures its organisation; eight central services are responsible for the conception, definition and evaluation of educational policies, while management functions are delegated to regional services.

1994

October

Changes to the framework for the continuous training of treachers (Decree Law 274/94)

November

Activities of trainers in labour-market programmes (Decree Law 66/94)

Annex IV

Calendar of main economic events

1994

March

The rate applicable to the overnight credit facility is increased from 11 per cent to 13 per cent.

The minimum wage is raised by 4 per cent to Esc 49 300 and by 4.9 per cent to Esc 43 000 for household services.

Social security contributions of employees of the public administrative sector are equalised with those of other dependant workers.

New legislation is introduced modifying the Value Added Tax to harmonise it with EU directives.

April

The Bank of Portugal suspends its regular intervention rates on the money market on 5 April. It resumes the regular liquidity injection operations on 19 April, with the rate at 11 per cent; the rate applicable to the overnight facility is set at 12 per cent.

New legislation eliminates withholding taxes on the interest earned on government securities held by non-residents, while establishing regulations governing the activities of those carrying out intermediation operations on the foreign exchange and money markets.

May

The Bank of Portugal reintroduces the regular liquidity absorption operations, with the rate at 10 per cent, and lowers in two steps the regular liquidity absorption and injections rates, to levels of 9.375 and 10.375 per cent, respectively; the rate on the daily facility is also lowered to 11.375 per cent. Regular interventions on the money market are suspended on 26 May.

June

New legislation introduces changes in the value added tax, as well as determining those government securities whose yields are exempted from the personal income and corporate tax, when purchased by non-residents.

A Special Market for Wholesale Transactions, intended for carrying out transactions of large blocks of bonds and other transferable securities, is created. In addition, the withholding tax on corporate bonds is cut by 5 points, thereby ending the preferential tax treatment for government bonds.

July

The Bank of Portugal introduces a standing facility for liquidity draining and repurchase agreements at variable rates for the regular supply of liquidity at a rate of 11 per cent; it resumes the overnight credit facility at a rate of 13.5 per cent. The liquidity-draining rate and the overnight credit facility rate are reduced in steps to 10.5 and 13 per cent, respectively.

August

The Bank of Portugal lowers in step the regular liquidity draining-rate and the overnight credit facility rate, to 9.25 and 12 per cent, respectively.

New legislation lays down the system regulating the information that credit institutions should provide to customers, as regards interest rates and other costs charged on credit operations. Non-residents issuing bonds and shares in Portugal, as well as residents issuing abroad, are no longer subject to the requirement of prior authorisation.

September

The Bank of Portugal lowers the regular liquidity-draining rate and the daily facility rate, to 8.75 and 11.5 per cent, respectively, and the rate of remuneration on required reserves to 8.75 per cent, effective as of 4 October 1994.

October

A new reserve requirement system is introduced, effective on 1 November 1994, lowering the reserve ratio from 17 per cent (partly remunerated) to 2 per cent (non-remunerated).

The first privatisation stage of *Banco de Fomento e Exterior, S.A.*, is approved.

The Bank of Portugal lowers the liquidity draining rate to 8.5 per cent.

November

A new legal system, governing transferable securities investment funds, is introduced.

December

The Budget for 1995 is approved.

A deposit insurance scheme is introduced.

1995

February

Introduction of calendar setting out the size, type and sequence of public debt issues.

STATISTICAL ANNEX AND STRUCTURAL INDICATORS

Table A. **Selected background statistics**

	Average 1984-93	1984	1985	1986	1987	1988	1989	1990	1991	1992	1993
A. Percentage changes											
Private consumption[1]	3.6	-2.9	0.7	6.3	6.0	5.7	3.6	6.9	5.2	4.3	0.4
Government consumption[1]	5.2	0.2	6.4	18.6	3.8	8.0	4.4	5.7	3.2	1.4	0.0
Gross fixed capital formation[1]	3.1	-17.4	-3.5	11.4	16.8	11.2	4.3	6.8	2.4	5.4	-6.3
Total domestic demand[1]	4.0	-6.7	0.9	8.8	9.5	9.6	4.4	6.4	3.9	4.7	-1.7
Exports of goods and services[1]	5.6	11.6	6.7	6.3	10.6	7.9	13.3	10.5	1.1	6.1	0.6
Imports of goods and services[1]	8.7	-4.4	1.4	17.3	20.2	16.5	7.9	13.7	4.9	11.1	-1.4
GDP[1]	3.0	-1.9	2.8	5.0	5.5	5.8	5.8	4.2	2.2	1.5	-0.9
GDP price deflator	14.6	24.6	21.8	19.5	11.1	10.9	11.4	13.0	14.3	13.0	6.4
Industrial production	3.0	2.3	0.9	7.3	4.3	3.9	6.8	9.1	-0.1	-2.6	-2.4
Employment	0.4	-0.1	-0.5	0.2	2.6	2.6	2.2	2.2	3.0	-6.4	-2.0
Compensation of employees (current prices)	16.8	18.2	20.7	20.0	16.6	16.6	17.9	20.8	19.3	12.4	5.7
Productivity (real GDP/employment)	2.6	-1.8	3.3	4.8	2.8	3.1	3.4	2.0	-0.8	8.5	1.0
Unit labour costs (compensation/real GDP)	13.5	20.5	17.4	14.3	10.5	10.2	11.5	15.9	16.7	10.7	6.9
B. Percentage ratios											
Gross fixed capital formation as per cent of GDP[1]	28.4	25.6	24.0	25.5	28.2	29.7	29.3	30.0	30.0	31.2	30.0
Stockbuilding as per cent of GDP[1]	-0.4	-3.3	-2.4	-2.8	-1.5	0.7	1.2	0.9	0.6	1.2	1.1
Foreign balance as per cent of GDP[1]	-13.3	-5.1	-3.4	-7.2	-11.2	-15.2	-13.7	-16.1	-18.0	-21.7	-21.7
Compensation of employees as per cent of GDP at current prices	48.2	50.9	49.4	47.4	46.6	47.2	47.0	48.0	49.2	48.1	48.1
Direct taxes as per cent of household income	6.0	5.2	5.5	4.9	4.3	5.5	6.5	6.2	6.9	7.9	7.0
Household saving as per cent of disposable income	18.4	27.7	24.6	22.3	21.8	17.6	16.3	15.2	14.3	11.9	12.2
Unemployment rate[2]	6.2	8.5	8.7	8.6	7.1	5.8	5.1	4.7	4.1	4.2	5.5
C. Other indicators											
Current balance (billion dollars)	-0.1	-0.6	0.3	1.2	0.4	-1.0	0.2	-0.2	-0.7	-0.2	-0.2

1. At constant prices.
2. Data based on the narrowest definition of unemployment.
Source: National Institute of Statistics (INE); Bank of Portugal; OECD estimates.

Table B. Expenditure on gross domestic product

Billion escudos

	1986	1987	1988	1989	1990	1991	1992	1993
A. At current prices								
Private consumption	3 241.5	3 767.8	4 437.5	5 140.4	6 141.8	7 244.5	8 346.9	8 971.8
Government consumption	718.4	830.7	1 020.8	1 226.7	1 495.6	1 810.8	2 142.0	2 338.5
Gross fixed investment	1 225.4	1 590.6	1 949.6	2 237.0	2 612.4	2 987.7	3 426.5	3 413.9
Stockbuilding	-45.9	42.1	152.3	117.7	116.4	100.0	117.4	94.8
Total domestic demand	5 139.4	6 231.2	7 560.2	8 721.8	10 366.2	12 143.0	14 032.8	14 819.0
Exports	1 467.4	1 793.1	2 128.3	2 681.0	3 131.9	3 218.8	3 266.1	3 522.1
Imports	1 580.9	2 132.7	2 778.9	3 262.3	3 908.5	4 177.7	4 470.2	4 715.6
GDP (at market prices)	5 025.9	5 891.6	6 909.6	8 140.5	9 589.6	11 184.1	12 828.7	13 625.5
B. At 1985 prices								
Private consumption	2 864.6	3 035.7	3 215.3	3 329.6	3 561.4	..	..	..
Government consumption	686.5	712.5	769.8	804.0	850.0	..	..	..
Gross fixed investment	1 072.7	1 252.6	1 392.4	1 452.3	1 550.6	..	..	..
Stockbuilding	-118.6	-68.3	33.0	59.0	48.8	..	..	..
Total domestic demand	4 505.2	4 932.5	5 410.6	5 644.9	6 010.8	..	..	..
Exports	1 404.9	1 553.8	1 668.5	1 891.1	2 088.8	..	..	..
Imports	1 704.9	2 048.1	2 384.0	2 570.9	2 922.3	..	..	..
GDP (at market prices)	4 205.2	4 438.2	4 695.1	4 965.0	5 177.3	..	..	..

Source: INE, *National Accounts* (1986-1989); Ministry of Finance (1990-1993).

Table C. **Household appropriation account**

Billion escudos

	1986	1987	1988	1989	1990	1991	1992	1993
Compensation of employees	2 225.9	2 588.7	3 014.0	3 556.6	4 289.3	4 967.0	5 702.1	5 975.8
Property and entrepreneurial income	1 754.1	1 931.2	2 144.4	2 427.4	2 961.5	3 544.9	4 048.3	4 104.9
Domestic transfers	601.1	756.2	865.5	997.8	1 239.3	1 561.5	1 884.8	2 184.4
Foreign transfers	394.5	485.5	529.5	597.6	644.2	672.6	647.7	625.7
Gross total income	4 975.6	5 761.6	6 553.4	7 579.4	9 134.3	10 746.0	12 282.9	12 890.8
Direct taxes	242.1	245.3	360.5	522.0	580.0	754.5	993.7	975.8
Social security contributions	574.7	690.5	792.0	930.9	1 122.7	1 337.1	1 569.8	1 712.7
Disposable income	4 158.8	4 825.8	5 400.9	6 126.5	7 431.6	8 654.4	9 719.4	10 202.3
Consumption	3 241.5	3 767.8	4 437.5	5 140.4	6 141.8	7 244.5	8 346.9	8 971.8

Source: INE, *National Accounts* (1986-1989); Ministry of Finance (1990-1993).

Table D. **General government account**

Billion escudos

	1987	1988	1989	1990	1991	1992	1993	1994
Current receipts	2 034.6	2 470.0	2 933.6	3 486.2	4 171.3	5 124.3	5 124.3	5 528.4
Direct taxes	327.6	477.1	678.3	805.7	1 024.9	1 291.3	1 243.8	1 318.5
Social security contributions	576.8	651.9	764.8	952.1	1 133.4	1 331.1	1 451.6	1 583.7
Indirect taxes	844.2	1 017.0	1 128.1	1 323.1	1 496.8	1 813.5	1 776.3	2 035.7
Other current receipts	286.0	324.1	362.5	405.3	516.2	688.4	652.6	592.5
Current expenditure	2 162.9	2 465.2	2 828.1	3 643.6	4 477.4	5 112.1	5 509.9	5 829.6
Expenditure on goods and services	830.7	1 020.8	1 226.7	1 495.6	1 955.7	2 241.1	2 415.7	2 601.0
Subsidies	123.6	128.1	122.0	147.1	120.6	130.6	135.9	117.4
Interest paid	462.9	491.4	519.7	832.4	944.6	991.3	908.9	848.6
Current transfers	745.7	824.9	959.6	1 168.6	1 456.5	1 749.0	2 049.4	2 262.5
Saving	-128.2	4.8	105.5	-157.4	-306.1	12.2	-385.6	-301.2
Capital receipts	102.8	118.7	176.7	227.1	256.4	379.8	447.2	415.2
Capital expenditure	306.3	373.8	470.7	593.6	686.4	818.1	1 023.3	969.0
Investment	196.4	250.9	281.8	328.9	423.1	523.3	571.1	646.9
Transfers	109.9	122.9	188.9	264.7	263.2	294.8	452.2	322.1
General government overall balance	-331.8	-250.3	-188.4	-524.0	-736.0	-426.1	-961.7	-855.0
(per cent of GDP)	-5.6	-3.6	-2.3	-5.5	-6.6	-3.3	-7.1	–
General government primary balance	131.1	241.1	331.3	308.4	208.6	565.3	-52.9	-6.4
(per cent of GDP)	2.2	3.5	4.1	3.2	1.9	4.4	-0.4	–
Memorandum:								
GDP	5 891.7	6 909.6	8 140.5	9 589.5	11 184.2	12 828.7	13 625.6	–

Source: INE (National account basis) for the period 1986 to 1990; Ministry of Finance for the period 1991 to 1994.

Table E. **Prices and wages**

Percentage changes

	1985	1986	1987	1988	1989	1990	1991	1992	1993	1994
Consumer prices [1]										
Total [2]	19.3	11.7	9.4	9.6	12.6	13.4	11.4	8.9	6.5	5.2
Food and drink	17.7	9.1	8.8	9.2	14.4	13.6	9.9	7.1	2.8	4.8
Clothing and footwear	23.3	23.5	15.8	13.2	10.5	9.5	11.9	11.9	7.0	4.1
Housing costs	20.0	10.7	7.4	10.1	11.8	11.9	12.1	9.6	7.0	3.5
Miscellanous	21.9	14.5	9.0	6.0	11.6	11.3	10.9	8.6	13.2	6.7
Wages in manufacturing industry										
Nominal	21.1	16.8	14.0	11.7	14.4	16.8	18.5	8.4	..	..
Real	1.5	4.6	4.2	1.8	1.6	3.0	6.4	-0.5	..	..

1. Mainland. New index as from 1988.
2. Excluding rent.
Source: INE; Bank of Portugal; OECD, *Main Economic Indicators.*

Table F. Civilian employment by sector[1]

Thousands

	1985	1986	1987	1988	1989	1990	1991	1992	1993	1994
Agriculture	968.5	890.3	925.9	885.4	829.0	795.3	799.1	490.1	482.3	490.2
Mining	23.5	27.2	26.6	28.5	33.6	35.8	30.6	22.3	19.6	17.5
Manufacturing	994.7	995.3	1 040.3	1 073.7	1 108.1	1 122.5	1 123.5	1 038.8	1 010.3	1 008.3
Construction	331.1	332.1	354.2	362.1	365.4	361.1	363.6	346.2	340.2	330.8
Electricity, gas and water	27.6	31.9	33.4	38.1	38.5	40.2	45.9	31.1	29.3	36.7
Transport and communication	176.3	174.0	167.7	176.9	183.0	201.7	220.7	210.1	198.9	196.4
Trade	562.9	598.6	584.6	629.9	666.9	692.0	742.2	857.9	825.6	817.3
Banking, insurance, real estate	117.1	127.0	132.1	139.5	154.5	203.6	211.2	137.3	140.9	134.9
Personal services	854.3	887.0	904.8	944.8	997.4	1 020.2	1 068.5	1 176.6	1 176.0	1 185.9
Total	4 056.0	4 063.4	4 169.6	4 278.9	4 376.4	4 472.4	4 605.3	4 310.4	4 223.1	4 218.0

1. From 1992, the data refers to 14 years and over population. Until 1991 the data refered to 12 years and over.
Source: OECD, Labour Force Statistics.

Table G. **Money supply and its counterparts**

Billion escudos at end of period

	1984	1985	1986	1987	1988	1989	1990	1991	1992	1993
Total money supply (L)	3 386	4 311	5 280	6 045	4 893	7 553	8 883	10 644	12 254	12 817
Money (M1–)	772	981	1 334	1 527	1 722	1 828	2 352	2 705	3 164	3 125
Notes and coins in circulation	267	319	399	458	510	577	624	683	708	692
Sight deposits of households										
and enterprises	805	662	935	1 069	1 213	1 251	1 728	2 022	2 456	2 433
Quasy money [1]	2 613	3 330	3 946	4 519	5 171	5 725	6 531	7 939	9 090	9 692
Counterparts										
Net foreign assets	774	973	935	1 181	1 827	2 512	2 716	3 447	3 753	4 418
Net lending to the public sector	901	1 349	1 866	2 332	2 616	2 546	2 797	2 823	3 136	3 201
Lending to the private sector	2 546	2 785	3 097	3 200	3 526	3 704	4 982	6 284	7 503	8 456
Miscellaneous, net	–834	–796	–618	–667	–1076	–1209	–1611	–1910	–2138	–3258

1. Including migrant deposits and Treasury bills.
Source: Bank of Portugal, *Quarterly Bulletin.*

Table H. **Breakdown by nationality for foreign visitors**

Thousands

	1984	1985	1986	1987	1988	1989	1990	1991	1992	1993
Total	9 811	11 692	13 057	16 173	16 077	16 471	18 422	19 641	20 742	20 579
Spain	7 309	8 798	9 960	12 583	12 124	12 186	13 806	14 583	15 553	15 776
United Kingdom	710	880	1 069	1 204	1 140	1 137	1 203	1 307	1 435	1 368
Germany	344	413	430	526	569	611	681	852	877	795
France	327	347	350	435	593	646	658	712	686	591
Netherlands	152	164	172	214	285	333	330	361	367	369
United States	209	230	150	195	223	235	252	178	220	208
Italy	72	93	109	134	155	185	221	291	283	265
Brazil	60	69	83	72	92	102	119	114	106	85
Canada	56	70	74	78	79	91	91	69	74	71
Sweden	72	54	69	70	87	95	98	114	108	94
Belgium	59	68	68	90	117	151	173	198	207	197
Switzerland	53	61	66	71	73	78	78	80	73	83
Other countries	389	444	457	502	540	621	713	782	753	677

Source: INE, *Bolletim mensal de estatistica.*

123

Table I. **Foreign trade by main commodity groups**

	1984	1985	1986	1987	1988	1989	1990	1991	1992	1993
Imports, total (million US$)	7 975.3	7 649.7	9 454.0	13 965.7	17 884.8	19 043.1	25 332.6	26 328.6	30 482.4	24 119.0
As a percentage of total										
Food and beverages	11.5	11.5	11.0	10.6	10.3	9.9	9.7	11.2	11.1	12.3
Basic metal and semi-finished goods	42.3	42.3	25.0	19.4	15.9	17.5	16.9	14.5	12.6	13.6
Manufactures	46.0	46.0	63.4	69.6	73.7	72.5	73.3	74.2	76.3	74.1
Chemicals	9.9	10.2	11.3	10.5	9.8	9.2	9.1	9.0	9.0	9.7
Goods classified chiefly by material	12.0	14.5	17.7	19.2	19.2	19.8	19.6	19.5	19.1	17.6
Machinery and transport equipmment	21.1	21.6	29.3	33.9	38.3	36.8	36.9	36.5	38.2	35.8
Miscellaneous	3.0	3.3	5.1	6.1	6.3	6.7	7.7	9.2	10.0	11.0
Unspecified	0.2	0.3	0.6	0.3	0.1	0.1	0.1	0.1	0.1	0.0
Exports, total (million US$)	5 207.5	5 685.4	7 204.9	9 318.3	10 989.7	12 797.7	16 415.7	16 326.1	18 540.6	15 403.4
As a percentage of total										
Food and beverages	8.8	7.8	8.2	7.3	7.7	7.0	6.6	7.3	7.0	6.8
Basic metal and semi-finished goods	15.2	14.5	12.2	11.9	12.8	14.0	12.8	10.5	9.9	9.6
Manufactures	75.3	76.0	78.4	80.1	79.1	78.6	80.3	81.9	82.9	83.5
Chemicals	7.7	7.0	6.1	5.4	6.0	5.6	5.2	4.6	4.2	4.4
Goods classified chiefly by material	28.1	27.7	26.4	25.4	25.4	23.7	23.4	24.1	23.4	23.7
Machinery and transport equipmment	17.3	15.6	15.7	16.5	16.7	19.1	19.6	19.7	21.6	21.1
Miscellaneous	22.2	25.7	30.3	32.8	31.0	30.3	32.1	33.6	33.6	34.4
Unspecified	0.8	1.7	1.2	0.7	0.4	0.4	0.3	0.3	0.2	0.1

Source: OECD, *Foreign Trade Statistics*, Series C.

Table J. **Geographical breakdown of foreign trade**[1]

	1985	1986	1987	1988	1989	1990	1991	1992	1993	1994
Exports, total (billion escudos)	950.4	1 055.0	1 304.1	1 598.1	2 035.5	2 255.6	2 405.2	2 475.2	2 546.0	2 658.2
As a percentage of total										
OECD countries	85.4	89.1	91.0	90.6	90.7	91.2	90.9	89.2	87.2	89.8
EU	62.6	68.3	71.1	72.0	71.8	73.9	75.4	75.0	73.1	74.8
Germany	13.8	14.7	15.4	14.7	15.7	16.7	19.1	19.1	19.7	18.6
France	12.7	15.2	15.8	15.2	15.0	15.5	14.4	14.2	14.7	14.7
Italy	4.0	3.9	3.9	4.2	4.3	4.1	4.0	3.9	2.9	3.3
United Kingdom	14.6	14.2	14.1	14.3	12.3	12.1	10.8	11.1	11.0	11.6
Spain	4.2	6.9	9.3	11.5	12.7	13.5	15.1	14.8	14.0	14.3
Other EU	13.4	13.3	12.6	12.1	11.8	11.9	12.0	11.8	11.4	12.1
United States	9.2	7.0	6.4	5.9	5.9	4.8	3.8	3.5	4.2	5.3
Other OECD countries	13.6	13.8	13.5	12.7	13.0	12.5	11.7	10.7	9.9	9.7
Non OECD countries	14.6	10.9	9.0	9.4	9.3	8.8	9.1	10.8	12.8	10.2
of which: OPEC	2.5	1.6	1.5	1.1	0.7	0.6	0.5	0.6	0.9	0.8
Previous Escudo Area	3.9	2.1	2.1	2.7	3.3	3.4	4.2	5.2	3.0	2.6
Imports, total (billion escudos)	1 281.3	1 399.4	1 955.1	2 596.7	3 033.4	3 467.6	3 893.7	4 087.6	3 882.8	3 966.7
As a percentage of total										
OECD countries	67.1	78.4	81.7	84.0	83.5	83.4	85.4	86.8	85.1	83.6
EU	46.1	58.9	63.8	67.3	68.2	69.2	72.0	73.8	71.8	70.3
Germany	11.7	14.4	15.1	14.7	14.6	14.4	15.0	15.1	15.0	13.9
France	8.0	10.0	11.2	11.5	11.7	11.5	11.9	12.9	12.7	12.1
Italy	5.1	7.9	8.7	9.3	9.1	10.0	10.2	10.2	8.7	8.5
United Kingdom	7.5	7.5	8.1	8.3	7.5	7.6	7.5	7.1	7.4	6.6
Spain	7.4	11.0	11.7	13.2	14.5	14.4	15.8	16.6	17.8	19.8
Other EU	6.3	8.2	8.9	10.3	10.8	11.3	11.5	11.9	10.1	9.3
United States	9.7	7.0	4.8	4.3	4.4	3.9	3.4	3.0	3.2	3.7
Other OECD countries	11.3	12.5	13.1	12.4	10.9	10.3	10.0	10.0	10.1	9.6
Non OECD countries	32.9	21.6	18.3	16.0	16.5	16.6	14.6	13.2	14.9	16.4
of which: OPEC	17.6	8.5	6.0	4.9	6.1	6.7	4.7	3.8	5.0	6.1
Previous Escudo Area	1.2	0.8	0.4	0.2	0.4	0.4	0.5	0.5	0.1	0.1

1. Data for 1994 refers to January-October.
Source: INE, *Bolletin mensal das estatisticas do commercio externo.*

125

Table K. **Balance of payments**

Million US dollars

	1984	1985	1986	1987	1988	1989	1990	1991	1992	1993
Exports, fob	5 172	5 679	7 263	9 262	10 874	12 744	16 299	16 199	18 188	15 428
Imports, fob	7 276	7 186	8 956	12 842	16 387	17 630	23 099	24 058	27 721	22 245
Trade balance	-2 104	-1 507	-1 693	-3 580	-5 513	-4 886	-6 800	-7 859	-9 533	-6 817
Services, net	-670	-380	-79	246	155	491	1 118	1 182	1 497	1 274
Travel	735	894	1 212	1 726	1 891	2 114	2 673	2 712	2 528	2 346
Transports	-187	-182	-131	-372	-584	-665	-888	-1 019	-1 073	-615
Investment income	-1 212	-1 165	-1 023	-934	-877	-719	-243	76	607	134
Government transactions	-77	-46	-100	-161	-172	-134	-192	-201	-181	-169
Other services	71	119	-37	-13	-103	-105	-232	-386	-384	-422
Transfers, net	2 189	2 234	2 934	3 778	4 333	4 559	5 496	6 011	7 824	6 703
Current balance	-585	347	1 162	444	-1 025	164	-186	-666	-212	1 160
Medium and long-term capital	1 227	1 091	-391	146	777	2 808	3 587	4 069	-613	2 539
Private	913	787	153	659	2 282	3 269	4 149	4 452	-555	568
Official	314	304	-544	-513	-1 505	-461	-562	-383	-58	1 971
Short-term and unrecorded	-360	-513	-1 103	1 333	1 871	1 101	589	1 735	1 452	-127
Non-monetary transactions, net	282	925	-332	1 923	1 623	4 073	3 990	5 138	627	3 572
Private monetary institutions short-term capital	-282	4	206	-107	-694	643	-330	785	-519	-3 852
Balance on official settlements	0	929	-126	1 816	929	4 716	3 660	5 923	108	-280
Use of IMF credit	227	0	0	-257	-498	0	0	0	0	0
Miscellaneous official accounts	-107	-205	1	-13	-18	16	5	-1	1	-2 408
Changes in reserve (increase = -)	-117	-723	125	-1 543	-411	-4 731	-3 667	-5 925	-106	2 691

Source : OECD.

126

Table L. Labour-market indicators

A. LABOUR MARKET PERFORMANCE

	Cyclical Peak: 1979	Cyclical Trough: 1984	1985	1992[1]	1993	1994
Standardised unemployment rate	6.1	8.5	8.7	4.2	5.7	7.1
Unemployment rate: Total	8.3	8.5	8.6	4.1	5.5	6.8
Male	4.3	5.9	6.4	3.5	4.7	6.0
Female	14.0	12.1	11.7	4.9	6.5	7.8
Youth[2]	14.6	19.9	20.1	9.9	12.7	14.7
Share of long-term unemployment in total unemployment[3]	..	47.0	53.0	25.9	29.3	34.1

B. STRUCTURAL OR INSTITUTIONAL CHARACTERISTICS

	1975	1980	1985	1992	1993	1994
Participation rate:[4] Total	64.5	67.8	67.9	68.4	67.7	67.5
Male	83.1	84.7	81.6	78.7	77.1	76.4
Female	48.0	52.9	55.2	58.9	59.0	59.3
Employment/population (15-64 years)	66.7	66.6	65.5	68.3	66.7	65.8
Non-wage labour costs[5] (as percentage of total compensation)	13.4	15.9	18.4	17.7	18.6	19.3
Unemployment insurance replacement ratio[6]	..	30.8	29.2	..	..	..
Minimum wage, non-agricultural sector (workers of 20 years and more, as percentage of the average earnings)	..	57.6	56.4	..	..	..

	1970/1960	1980/1970	1985/1980	1991/1986	1994/1992
Average percentage changes (annual rates)[8]					
Labour force (15-64 years)	0.5	2.0	0.7	1.9	1.9
Employment: Total	0.4	1.4	0.5	2.8	2.8
Industries	0.7	2.7	-0.9	3.1	3.1
Services	4.3	1.4	3.8	5.3	5.3

1. Break in series.
2. People between 15 and 24 years as a percentage of the labour force of the same age group.
3. Persons seeking a job for 12 months and over as a percentage of total unemployed.
4. Labour force (in 1975, civil labour force) as a percentage of relevant population group, aged between 15 and 64 years.
5. In 1975 civil employment.
6. Employers' contributions to social security and pension funds. 1992,1993, 1994 are estimates based on National Accounts (1986 basis).
7. Unemployment benefits per unemployed as a percentage of compensation per employee.
8. 1960 and 1970, National Accounts. 1980, 1985, 1986 and 1991, Employment Survey.
Source: INE, DEP/MESS.

Table M. **Public sector**

Per cent of GDP

A. BUDGET INDICATORS: GENERAL GOVERNMENT ACCOUNT

	1970	1980	1985	1990
Current receipts	25.6	31.4	35.9	44.1
Non-interest expenditure	22.8	36.4	36.8	43.6
Primary budget balance	3.3	-4.8	-0.4	4.3
Interest payments	0.5	3.1	8.1	9.1
General government budget balance	2.8	-7.9	-8.5	-4.7

B. THE STRUCTURE OF GENERAL GOVERNMENT EXPENDITURE

	1970	1980	1985	1990
Total expenditure	23.4	39.5	44.8	52.6
of which:				
Current consumption	14.0	14.5	14.3	18.3
Transfers to persons	4.0	10.7	12.8	15.5
Subsidies	1.5	5.2	4.1	1.4
Capital formation	2.5	4.1	3.1	4.3

Source: OECD.

Table N. Production and employment structures

	Per cent share of GDP at factor costs (current prices)					Per cent share of total employment				
	1977[1]	1980[1]	1985[1]	1990[1]	1990[2]	1977[1]	1980[1]	1985[1]	1990[1]	1990[2]
Agriculture, forestry and fishing	11.9	10.3	8.0	5.8	6.8	31.8	27.2	25.4	20.3	17.7
Manufacturing	27.9	31.0	30.4	27.9	26.2	23.6	25.1	24.3	23.8	25.0
of which:										
Food, beverages and tobacco	5.7	5.7	6.1	6.0	5.4	3.5	3.3	3.2	3.3	2.7
Textiles, clothing, leather	5.4	7.0	7.8	7.2	6.0	7.6	8.1	8.3	8.3	8.8
Wood, paper and paper products	3.4	3.7	3.2	3.1	2.8	3.1	3.2	2.9	2.7	2.9
Chemicals and products of petroleum, coal, rubber, etc.	3.0	2.8	3.3	2.1	2.1	1.5	1.7	1.6	1.5	1.2
Non-metallic mineral products except products of petroleum and coal	2.4	2.6	2.1	1.9	0.6	1.8	1.9	1.7	1.7	0.6
Fabricated metal products, machinery and equipment	5.6	6.8	5.6	4.9	4.1	4.0	4.5	4.2	3.9	4.2
Electricity, gas and water	1.9	2.1	3.5	3.1	4.1	0.6	0.8	0.9	0.8	0.9
Construction	7.7	7.1	5.7	6.9	5.2	9.5	10.1	9.5	9.9	8.4
Services	50.6	49.5	52.5	56.4	57.6	34.4	36.8	39.9	45.2	48.0
of which:										
Wholesale and retail trade, restaurants and hotels	21.4	21.7	22.4	19.8	15.4	13.0	13.4	13.6	17.2	16.5
Transport, storage and communication	5.6	5.5	7.7	5.4	6.7	4.6	4.5	4.4	4.4	3.9
Finance, insurance, real estate and business services	10.7	10.5	10.1	13.1	14.6	2.2	2.6	3.0	3.2	4.3

1. National accounts, base = 1966.
2. National accounts, base = 1977.
Source: OECD, *National Accounts.*

BASIC STATISTICS

BASIC STATISTICS:

INTERNATIONAL COMPARISONS

	Units	Reference period [1]	Australia	A
Population				
Total	Thousands	1992	17 489	7
Inhabitants per sq. km	Number	1992	2	
Net average annual increase over previous 10 years	%	1992	1.4	
Employment				
Civilian employment (CE) [2]	Thousands	1992	7 637	3
Of which: Agriculture	% of CE		5.3	
Industry	% of CE		23.8	
Services	% of CE		71	
Gross domestic product (GDP)				
At current prices and current exchange rates	Bill. US$	1992	296.6	1
Per capita	US$		16 959	23
At current prices using current PPPs [3]	Bill. US$	1992	294.5	
Per capita	US$		16 800	18
Average annual volume growth over previous 5 years	%	1992	2	
Gross fixed capital formation (GFCF)	% of GDP	1992	19.7	
Of which: Machinery and equipment	% of GDP		9.3	
Residential construction	% of GDP		5.1	
Average annual volume growth over previous 5 years	%	1992	−1	
Gross saving ratio [4]	% of GDP	1992	15.6	
General government				
Current expenditure on goods and services	% of GDP	1992	18.5	
Current disbursements [5]	% of GDP	1992	36.9	
Current receipts	% of GDP	1992	33.1	
Net official development assistance	% of GNP	1992	0.33	
Indicators of living standards				
Private consumption per capita using current PPPs [3]	US$	1992	10 527	9
Passenger cars, per 1 000 inhabitants	Number	1990	430	
Telephones, per 1 000 inhabitants	Number	1990	448	
Television sets, per 1 000 inhabitants	Number	1989	484	
Doctors, per 1 000 inhabitants	Number	1991	2	
Infant mortality per 1 000 live births	Number	1991	7.1	
Wages and prices (average annual increase over previous 5 years)				
Wages (earnings or rates according to availability)	%	1992	5	
Consumer prices	%	1992	5.2	
Foreign trade				
Exports of goods, fob*	Mill. US$	1992	42 844	44
As % of GDP	%		14.4	
Average annual increase over previous 5 years	%		10.1	
Imports of goods, cif*	Mill. US$	1992	40 751	54
As % of GDP	%		13.7	
Average annual increase over previous 5 years	%		8.6	
Total official reserves [6]	Mill. SDRs	1992	8 152	9
As ratio of average monthly imports of goods	Ratio		2.4	

* At current prices and exchange rates.
1. Unless otherwise stated.
2. According to the definitions used in OECD *Labour Force Statistics*.
3. PPPs = Purchasing Power Parities.
4. Gross saving = Gross national disposable income minus private and government consumption.
5. Current disbursements = Current expenditure on goods and services plus current transfers and payments of property income.
6. Gold included in reserves is valued at 35 SDRs per ounce. End of year.
7. Including Luxembourg.

EMPLOYMENT OPPORTUNITIES

Economics Department, OECD

The Economics Department of the OECD offers challenging and rewarding opportunities to economists interested in applied policy analysis in an international environment. The Department's concerns extend across the entire field of economic policy analysis, both macroeconomic and microeconomic. Its main task is to provide, for discussion by committees of senior officials from Member countries, documents and papers dealing with current policy concerns. Within this programme of work, three major responsibilities are:

- to prepare regular surveys of the economies of individual Member countries;
- to issue full twice-yearly reviews of the economic situation and prospects of the OECD countries in the context of world economic trends;
- to analyse specific policy issues in a medium-term context for the OECD as a whole, and to a lesser extent for the non-OECD countries.

The documents prepared for these purposes, together with much of the Department's other economic work, appear in published form in the *OECD Economic Outlook, OECD Economic Surveys, OECD Economic Studies* and the Department's *Working Papers* series.

The Department maintains a world econometric model, INTERLINK, which plays an important role in the preparation of the policy analyses and twice-yearly projections. The availability of extensive cross-country data bases and good computer resources facilitates comparative empirical analysis, much of which is incorporated into the model.

The Department is made up of about 80 professional economists from a variety of backgrounds and Member countries. Most projects are carried out by small teams and last from four to eighteen months. Within the Department, ideas and points of view are widely discussed; there is a lively professional interchange, and all professional staff have the opportunity to contribute actively to the programme of work.

Skills the Economics Department is looking for:

a) Solid competence in using the tools of both microeconomic and macroeconomic theory to answer policy questions. Experience indicates that this normally requires the equivalent of a Ph.D. in economics or substantial relevant professional experience to compensate for a lower degree.

b) Solid knowledge of economic statistics and quantitative methods; this includes how to identify data, estimate structural relationships, apply basic techniques of time series analysis, and test hypotheses. It is essential to be able to interpret results sensibly in an economic policy context.

c) A keen interest in and extensive knowledge of policy issues, economic developments and their political/social contexts.

d) Interest and experience in analysing questions posed by policy-makers and presenting the results to them effectively and judiciously. Thus, work experience in government agencies or policy research institutions is an advantage.

e) The ability to write clearly, effectively, and to the point. The OECD is a bilingual organisation with French and English as the official languages. Candidates must have excellent knowledge of one of these languages, and some knowledge of the other. Knowledge of other languages might also be an advantage for certain posts.

f) For some posts, expertise in a particular area may be important, but a successful candidate is expected to be able to work on a broader range of topics relevant to the work of the Department. Thus, except in rare cases, the Department does not recruit narrow specialists.

g) The Department works on a tight time schedule with strict deadlines. Moreover, much of the work in the Department is carried out in small groups. Thus, the ability to work with other economists from a variety of cultural and professional backgrounds, to supervise junior staff, and to produce work on time is important.

General information

The salary for recruits depends on educational and professional background. Positions carry a basic salary from FF 305 700 or FF 377 208 for Administrators (economists) and from FF 438 348 for Principal Administrators (senior economists). This may be supplemented by expatriation and/or family allowances, depending on nationality, residence and family situation. Initial appointments are for a fixed term of two to three years.

Vacancies are open to candidates from OECD Member countries. The Organisation seeks to maintain an appropriate balance between female and male staff and among nationals from Member countries.

For further information on employment opportunities in the Economics Department, contact:

Administrative Unit
Economics Department
OECD
2, rue André-Pascal
75775 PARIS CEDEX 16
FRANCE

E-Mail: compte.esadmin@oecd.org

Applications citing "ECSUR", together with a detailed *curriculum vitae* in English or French, should be sent to the Head of Personnel at the above address.

MAIN SALES OUTLETS OF OECD PUBLICATIONS
PRINCIPAUX POINTS DE VENTE DES PUBLICATIONS DE L'OCDE

ARGENTINA – ARGENTINE
Carlos Hirsch S.R.L.
Galería Güemes, Florida 165, 4° Piso
1333 Buenos Aires   Tel. (1) 331.1787 y 331.2391
                     Telefax: (1) 331.1787

AUSTRALIA – AUSTRALIE
D.A. Information Services
648 Whitehorse Road, P.O.B 163
Mitcham, Victoria 3132   Tel. (03) 873.4411
                          Telefax: (03) 873.5679

AUSTRIA – AUTRICHE
Gerold & Co.
Graben 31
Wien I   Tel. (0222) 533.50.14
                   Telefax: (0222) 512.47.31.29

BELGIUM – BELGIQUE
Jean De Lannoy
Avenue du Roi 202
B-1060 Bruxelles   Tel. (02) 538.51.69/538.08.41
                           Telefax: (02) 538.08.41

CANADA
Renouf Publishing Company Ltd.
1294 Algoma Road
Ottawa, ON K1B 3W8   Tel. (613) 741.4333
                          Telefax: (613) 741.5439
Stores:
61 Sparks Street
Ottawa, ON K1P 5R1   Tel. (613) 238.8985
211 Yonge Street
Toronto, ON M5B 1M4   Tel. (416) 363.3171
                       Telefax: (416)363.59.63

Les Éditions La Liberté Inc.
3020 Chemin Sainte-Foy
Sainte-Foy, PQ G1X 3V6   Tel. (418) 658.3763
                           Telefax: (418) 658.3763

Federal Publications Inc.
165 University Avenue, Suite 701
Toronto, ON M5H 3B8   Tel. (416) 860.1611
                           Telefax: (416) 860.1608

Les Publications Fédérales
1185 Université
Montréal, QC H3B 3A7   Tel. (514) 954.1633
                           Telefax: (514) 954.1635

CHINA – CHINE
China National Publications Import
Export Corporation (CNPIEC)
16 Gongti E. Road, Chaoyang District
P.O. Box 88 or 50
Beijing 100704 PR   Tel. (01) 506.6688
                          Telefax: (01) 506.3101

CHINESE TAIPEI – TAIPEI CHINOIS
Good Faith Worldwide Int'l. Co. Ltd.
9th Floor, No. 118, Sec. 2
Chung Hsiao E. Road
Taipei   Tel. (02) 391.7396/391.7397
                          Telefax: (02) 394.9176

**CZECH REPUBLIC – RÉPUBLIQUE
  TCHÈQUE**
Artia Pegas Press Ltd.
Narodni Trida 25
POB 825
111 21 Praha 1   Tel. 26.65.68
                              Telefax: 26.20.81

DENMARK – DANEMARK
Munksgaard Book and Subscription Service
35, Nørre Søgade, P.O. Box 2148
DK-1016 København K   Tel. (33) 12.85.70
                           Telefax: (33) 12.93.87

EGYPT – ÉGYPTE
Middle East Observer
41 Sherif Street
Cairo   Tel. 392.6919
                              Telefax: 360-6804

FINLAND – FINLANDE
Akateeminen Kirjakauppa
Keskuskatu 1, P.O. Box 128
00100 Helsinki
Subscription Services/Agence d'abonnements :
P.O. Box 23
00371 Helsinki   Tel. (358 0) 12141
                          Telefax: (358 0) 121.4450

FRANCE
OECD/OCDE
Mail Orders/Commandes par correspondance:
2, rue André-Pascal
75775 Paris Cedex 16   Tel. (33-1) 45.24.82.00
                      Telefax: (33-1) 49.10.42.76
                            Telex: 640048 OCDE
Orders via Minitel, France only/
Commandes par Minitel, France exclusivement :
36 15 OCDE

OECD Bookshop/Librairie de l'OCDE :
33, rue Octave-Feuillet
75016 Paris   Tel. (33-1) 45.24.81.81
                            (33-1) 45.24.81.67

Documentation Française
29, quai Voltaire
75007 Paris   Tel. 40.15.70.00

Gibert Jeune (Droit-Économie)
6, place Saint-Michel
75006 Paris   Tel. 43.25.91.19

Librairie du Commerce International
10, avenue d'Iéna
75016 Paris   Tel. 40.73.34.60

Librairie Dunod
Université Paris-Dauphine
Place du Maréchal de Lattre de Tassigny
75016 Paris   Tel. (1) 44.05.40.13

Librairie Lavoisier
11, rue Lavoisier
75008 Paris   Tel. 42.65.39.95

Librairie L.G.D.J. - Montchrestien
20, rue Soufflot
75005 Paris   Tel. 46.33.89.85

Librairie des Sciences Politiques
30, rue Saint-Guillaume
75007 Paris   Tel. 45.48.36.02

P.U.F.
49, boulevard Saint-Michel
75005 Paris   Tel. 43.25.83.40

Librairie de l'Université
12a, rue Nazareth
13100 Aix-en-Provence   Tel. (16) 42.26.18.08

Documentation Française
165, rue Garibaldi
69003 Lyon   Tel. (16) 78.63.32.23

Librairie Decitre
29, place Bellecour
69002 Lyon   Tel. (16) 72.40.54.54

Librairie Sauramps
Le Triangle
34967 Montpellier Cedex 2   Tel. (16) 67.58.85.15
                        Tekefax: (16) 67.58.27.36

GERMANY – ALLEMAGNE
OECD Publications and Information Centre
August-Bebel-Allee 6
D-53175 Bonn   Tel. (0228) 959.120
                      Telefax: (0228) 959.12.17

GREECE – GRÈCE
Librairie Kauffmann
Mavrokordatou 9
106 78 Athens   Tel. (01) 32.55.321
                       Telefax: (01) 32.30.320

HONG-KONG
Swindon Book Co. Ltd.
Astoria Bldg. 3F
34 Ashley Road, Tsimshatsui
Kowloon, Hong Kong   Tel. 2376.2062
                         Telefax: 2376.0685

HUNGARY – HONGRIE
Euro Info Service
Margitsziget, Európa Ház
1138 Budapest   Tel. (1) 111.62.16
                       Telefax: (1) 111.60.61

ICELAND – ISLANDE
Mál Mog Menning
Laugavegi 18, Pósthólf 392
121 Reykjavik   Tel. (1) 552.4240
                       Telefax: (1) 562.3523

INDIA – INDE
Oxford Book and Stationery Co.
Scindia House
New Delhi 110001   Tel. (11) 331.5896/5308
                      Telefax: (11) 332.5993

17 Park Street
Calcutta 700016   Tel. 240832

INDONESIA – INDONÉSIE
Pdii-Lipi
P.O. Box 4298
Jakarta 12042   Tel. (21) 573.34.67
                       Telefax: (21) 573.34.67

IRELAND – IRLANDE
Government Supplies Agency
Publications Section
4/5 Harcourt Road
Dublin 2   Tel. 661.31.11
                          Telefax: 475.27.60

ISRAEL
Praedicta
5 Shatner Street
P.O. Box 34030
Jerusalem 91430   Tel. (2) 52.84.90/1/2
                         Telefax: (2) 52.84.93

R.O.Y. International
P.O. Box 13056
Tel Aviv 61130   Tel. (3) 49.61.08
                       Telefax: (3) 544.60.39

Palestinian Authority/Middle East:
INDEX Information Services
P.O.B. 19502
Jerusalem   Tel. (2) 27.12.19
                       Telefax: (2) 27.16.34

ITALY – ITALIE
Libreria Commissionaria Sansoni
Via Duca di Calabria 1/1
50125 Firenze   Tel. (055) 64.54.15
                       Telefax: (055) 64.12.57

Via Bartolini 29
20155 Milano   Tel. (02) 36.50.83

Editrice e Libreria Herder
Piazza Montecitorio 120
00186 Roma   Tel. 679.46.28
                         Telefax: 678.47.51

Libreria Hoepli
Via Hoepli 5
20121 Milano   Tel. (02) 86.54.46
                       Telefax: (02) 805.28.86

Libreria Scientifica
Dott. Lucio de Biasio 'Aeiou'
Via Coronelli, 6
20146 Milano   Tel. (02) 48.95.45.52
                       Telefax: (02) 48.95.45.48

JAPAN – JAPON
OECD Publications and Information Centre
Landic Akasaka Building
2-3-4 Akasaka, Minato-ku
Tokyo 107   Tel. (81.3) 3586.2016
                       Telefax: (81.3) 3584.7929

KOREA – CORÉE
Kyobo Book Centre Co. Ltd.
P.O. Box 1658, Kwang Hwa Moon
Seoul   Tel. 730.78.91
                         Telefax: 735.00.30

MALAYSIA – MALAISIE
University of Malaya Bookshop
University of Malaya
P.O. Box 1127, Jalan Pantai Baru
59700 Kuala Lumpur
Malaysia   Tel. 756.5000/756.5425
                                        Telefax: 756.3246

MEXICO – MEXIQUE
Revistas y Periodicos Internacionales S.A. de C.V.
Florencia 57 - 1004
Mexico, D.F. 06600   Tel. 207.81.00
                                        Telefax: 208.39.79

NETHERLANDS – PAYS-BAS
SDU Uitgeverij Plantijnstraat
Externe Fondsen
Postbus 20014
2500 EA's-Gravenhage   Tel. (070) 37.89.880
Voor bestellingen: Telefax: (070) 34.75.778

**NEW ZEALAND
NOUVELLE-ZÉLANDE**
Legislation Services
P.O. Box 12418
Thorndon, Wellington   Tel. (04) 496.5652
                                        Telefax: (04) 496.5698

NORWAY – NORVÈGE
Narvesen Info Center – NIC
Bertrand Narvesens vei 2
P.O. Box 6125 Etterstad
0602 Oslo 6   Tel. (022) 57.33.00
                                        Telefax: (022) 68.19.01

PAKISTAN
Mirza Book Agency
65 Shahrah Quaid-E-Azam
Lahore 54000   Tel. (42) 353.601
                                        Telefax: (42) 231.730

PHILIPPINE – PHILIPPINES
International Book Center
5th Floor, Filipinas Life Bldg.
Ayala Avenue
Metro Manila   Tel. 81.96.76
                                Telex 23312 RHP PH

PORTUGAL
Livraria Portugal
Rua do Carmo 70-74
Apart. 2681
1200 Lisboa   Tel. (01) 347.49.82/5
                                        Telefax: (01) 347.02.64

SINGAPORE – SINGAPOUR
Gower Asia Pacific Pte Ltd.
Golden Wheel Building
41, Kallang Pudding Road, No. 04-03
Singapore 1334   Tel. 741.5166
                                        Telefax: 742.9356

SPAIN – ESPAGNE
Mundi-Prensa Libros S.A.
Castelló 37, Apartado 1223
Madrid 28001   Tel. (91) 431.33.99
                                        Telefax: (91) 575.39.98

Libreria Internacional AEDOS
Consejo de Ciento 391
08009 – Barcelona   Tel. (93) 488.30.09
                                        Telefax: (93) 487.76.59

Llibreria de la Generalitat
Palau Moja
Rambla dels Estudis, 118
08002 – Barcelona
                (Subscripcions) Tel. (93) 318.80.12
                (Publicacions) Tel. (93) 302.67.23
                                        Telefax: (93) 412.18.54

SRI LANKA
Centre for Policy Research
c/o Colombo Agencies Ltd.
No. 300-304, Galle Road
Colombo 3   Tel. (1) 574240, 573551-2
                                Telefax: (1) 575394, 510711

SWEDEN – SUÈDE
Fritzes Customer Service
S–106 47 Stockholm   Tel. (08) 690.90.90
                                        Telefax: (08) 20.50.21

Subscription Agency/Agence d'abonnements :
Wennergren-Williams Info AB
P.O. Box 1305
171 25 Solna   Tel. (08) 705.97.50
                                        Telefax: (08) 27.00.71

SWITZERLAND – SUISSE
Maditec S.A. (Books and Periodicals - Livres
et périodiques)
Chemin des Palettes 4
Case postale 266
1020 Renens VD 1   Tel. (021) 635.08.65
                                        Telefax: (021) 635.07.80

Librairie Payot S.A.
4, place Pépinet
CP 3212
1002 Lausanne   Tel. (021) 341.33.47
                                        Telefax: (021) 341.33.45

Librairie Unilivres
6, rue de Candolle
1205 Genève   Tel. (022) 320.26.23
                                        Telefax: (022) 329.73.18

Subscription Agency/Agence d'abonnements :
Dynapresse Marketing S.A.
38 avenue Vibert
1227 Carouge   Tel. (022) 308.07.89
                                        Telefax: (022) 308.07.99

See also – Voir aussi :
OECD Publications and Information Centre
August-Bebel-Allee 6
D-53175 Bonn (Germany)   Tel. (0228) 959.120
                                        Telefax: (0228) 959.12.17

THAILAND – THAÏLANDE
Suksit Siam Co. Ltd.
113, 115 Fuang Nakhon Rd.
Opp. Wat Rajbopith
Bangkok 10200   Tel. (662) 225.9531/2
                                        Telefax: (662) 222.5188

TURKEY – TURQUIE
Kültür Yayinlari Is-Türk Ltd. Sti.
Atatürk Bulvari No. 191/Kat 13
Kavaklidere/Ankara   Tel. 428.11.40 Ext. 2458
Dolmabahce Cad. No. 29
Besiktas/Istanbul   Tel. 260.71.88
                                        Telex: 43482B

UNITED KINGDOM – ROYAUME-UNI
HMSO
Gen. enquiries   Tel. (071) 873 0011
Postal orders only:
P.O. Box 276, London SW8 5DT
Personal Callers HMSO Bookshop
49 High Holborn, London WC1V 6HB
                                        Telefax: (071) 873 8200
Branches at: Belfast, Birmingham, Bristol,
Edinburgh, Manchester

UNITED STATES – ÉTATS-UNIS
OECD Publications and Information Center
2001 L Street N.W., Suite 650
Washington, D.C. 20036-4910 Tel. (202) 785.6323
                                        Telefax: (202) 785.0350

VENEZUELA
Libreria del Este
Avda F. Miranda 52, Aptdo. 60337
Edificio Galipán
Caracas 106   Tel. 951.1705/951.2307/951.1297
                                Telegram: Libreste Caracas

Subscription to OECD periodicals may also be
placed through main subscription agencies.

Les abonnements aux publications périodiques de
l'OCDE peuvent être souscrits auprès des
principales agences d'abonnement.

Orders and inquiries from countries where Distribu-
tors have not yet been appointed should be sent to:
OECD Publications Service, 2 rue André-Pascal,
75775 Paris Cedex 16, France.

Les commandes provenant de pays où l'OCDE n'a
pas encore désigné de distributeur peuvent être
adressées à : OCDE, Service des Publications,
2, rue André-Pascal, 75775 Paris Cedex 16, France.

5-1995